COVER
$15.33

BJS
$9.99

BJS # 607762

27342 21286   1

W9-BIU-321

Alan Aldridge for the Beatles' song Being for the Benefit of Mr Kite.

SIXTIES
SOURCE
BOOK

NIGEL CAWTHORNE

CHARTWELL
BOOKS, INC.

A QUARTO BOOK

Published by Chartwell Books
A Division of Book Sales, Inc.
110 Enterprise Avenue
Secaucus, New Jersey 07094

Copyright © 1989 Quarto Publishing plc
All rights reserved. No part of this publication
may be reproduced, stored in a retrieval system
or transmitted in any form or by any means,
electronic, mechanical, photocopying, recording
or otherwise, without the permission of the
copyright holder.

ISBN 1-55521-529-7

This book was designed and produced by
Quarto Publishing plc
The Old Brewery, 6 Blundell Street
London N7 9BH

This book is sold subject to the condition that it shall not, by way of trade or
otherwise, be lent, re-sold, hired out or otherwise circulated without the
publisher's prior consent in any form of binding or cover other than that in which
it is published and without a similar condition including this condition being
imposed upon the subsequent purchaser.

Senior editor Kate Kirby
Editor Richard Dawes

Designer Peter Bridgewater

Editorial director Carolyn King
Art director Moira Clinch
Assistant art director Chloë Alexander

Typeset by Ampersand Typesetters, Bournemouth
Manufactured in Hong Kong by Regent Publishing Services Ltd
Printed in Hong Kong by South Sea Int'l Press Ltd.

Special thanks to Arlene Bridgewater and Nick Law

CONTENTS

FOREWORD

People were different in the sixties. They were more tolerant of women, minority groups, and the gay community. And they were less conservative. But I suppose more people had the money to be able to indulge liberal ideas. Many did not have to bother with earning a living or running a business. When I started out in the sixties it was almost embarrassing to be making money out of running a business.

I guess our liberal, progressive ideas came from people like John Lennon. Though I was working and had no time to sit around listening to music, somehow what Lennon and the others had to say filtered through to me.

The idealism of figures like Martin Luther King and John F. Kennedy was also influential, and I remember a boy coming into our school dormitory in tears the day President Kennedy was shot. But we were too young to appreciate what it really meant. We thought the bomb was about to be dropped. Politicians of whatever colour were distant. It was the voice of the musicians that people listened to back then.

Vietnam was crucial, too. In 1968, I was in Grosvenor Square with Vanessa Redgrave, Tariq Ali and David Hemmings during that huge protest. And I spoke out against the war with French radical Danny Cohn-Bendit – the leader of the student revolt at the Sorbonne that same year – outside University College, London, but I fluffed my lines.

In the early sixties, I was too young to be a mod or a rocker – I was only ten in 1960 and grew up, through my teens, with the decade. I was influenced by the hippy thing, although, when you are working, there is no time to sit around smoking dope. I knew *Oz* editor Richard Neville and I suppose he could get away with it. But *Student*, the magazine I ran during the late sixties, was not really "alternative" in the same way.

There was a great sense of optimism. You could do anything if you set your mind to it. We were also very concerned about people. I started the Student Advisory Centre, which is now called Help. My girlfriend had got pregnant and I realized how difficult it was for most young people to handle problems like that, especially if they had come straight to London from the country. We set up the SAC in the crypt of a church in Bayswater, working on two coffins and a marble slab. Not many people would begin in such a disorganized fashion now.

Overall, I feel that I missed out on the sixties, along with others who really were there. I was too busy to notice what was going on. I acknowledge, though, that I am a product of that time. It is a decade that – more than any other – has left its enduring mark, on me and everything around us. You will never understand the eighties – or the nineties – unless you understand the sixties first.

Richard Branson

INTRODUCTION

The sixties began with presidential hopeful Jack Kennedy and an *Itsy Bitsy Teenie Weenie Yellow Polkadot Bikini.* It ended with Charles Manson singing *Helter Skelter,* the Mylai massacre tracked in Lieutenant William Calley's tears and with the young Black Meredith Hunter who *Let It Bleed* at Altamont. After three days of love and peace at Woodstock earlier in the year, he was stabbed by Hell's Angels employed by the Rolling Stones as security at a free "Thank You America" concert in California at the end of their US tour.

The hunger for change

Meanwhile the sixties had been to San Francisco, Marrakesh, the moon. They had swung in London, rioted in Paris, built a wall in Berlin, bombed Vietnam back to the Stone Age, starved in Biafra, seceded in Katanga, declared UDI in Rhodesia, seen a Prague Spring, a missile crisis in Cuba and a cultural revolution in China (and almost everywhere else).

The decade had grown its hair long, taken purple hearts, smoked pot, dropped acid, kissed the sky in a Saturn 5, dreamed a dream with Martin Luther King, taken the Pill, sat in at lunch counters, been jailed with Norman Mailer and Nelson Mandela, done the twist in the White House, ridden to freedom across the Deep South, taken its clothes off on stage, wasted gooks from the Delta to the DMZ and done its own thing at a love-in and a happening. During the decade, sex had been invented. Negroes became Blacks. Four lads from Liverpool became more famous than Jesus Christ. Camelot began its slow transmogrification into Watergate. The Earth had truly been seen as one planet, by men in space. Even the traffic lights threatened to turn blue tomorrow.

A pocketful of dollars

The sixties were a tumbling, tumultuous, torrent of a decade. Their irrepressible optimism stemmed from the baby boom and a thriving world economy fuelled by American production during World War II and the Marshall Plan which poured millions of US dollars into a war-shattered Europe. The generation conceived in the first flush of victory had money in their pockets. And there would soon be more where that came from, once the US space programme, the welfare revolution of LBJ's Great Society and the Vietnam war got underway.

A new world was being forged in the white heat of the technological revolution. Mankind was reaching out into space. New countries in Africa, Asia and the Caribbean were achieving nationhood while their European former masters were finding a new role in the world for themselves. Blacks in the United States asserted themselves for the first time too. Their protest and their music set the world on fire. Everywhere youth was throwing off the old staid ways of the older generation to the raucous

1 The election of President John F. Kennedy in 1960 at the age of 43, seen here with his glamorous young wife, epitomized the new youthful spirit of hope that was born in the sixties. Even Kennedy's assassination in November 1963 did not cause that spirit to falter.

2 The freethinking spirit of the age even spread to the East. Unofficially, Czechoslovak communism briefly assumed a human face during the "Prague Spring". But this manifestation of liberalism was crushed by the tanks of the Soviet Union. Four other Warsaw Pact nations came to the fraternal assistance of Czechoslovakia on 21 August, 1968.

3 The youthful optimism of the sixties was from the start fired by pop music and especially by four mop-topped youths from Liverpool. Their music swept the world and their sexual values, interest in Eastern religions, use of drugs, style of dress, adoption of hippy ideals and advocacy of peace in Vietnam were all influential.

4 The Beatles' faces appeared everywhere. Here they are seen on two polka-dot shift dresses. These were designed to be worn by usherettes at the group's concert at the Granada Theatre, Bedford, in England in 1964.

5 Black and white people came together in America in the sixties to fight injustice.

3

4

5

6 Harold Wilson, Britain's Prime Minister from 1964 to 1970, despite his grey hair, cultivated a youthful Kennedy-esque image. His great advantage in the eyes of young voters and all those concerned with the destiny of the working class was that his constituency was in Liverpool, home of the Beatles and innumerable other groups, and a real, working city.

6

sound of rock and roll.

On 31 January 1960, a senator barely known outside Massachusetts, John F. Kennedy, declared his candidacy in the US presidential race. Vice President Richard Nixon had already tossed his hat into the ring on 9 January. Together they were to stage the first presidential debate to be aired on TV. It is said that those who heard the debate on radio declared Nixon – with his clear command of the facts and compelling arguments – the winner by a long length. Those who saw the debate on TV thought the younger man – the suave, handsome Kennedy – the winner over the sweating, shifty, ill-shaven Nixon. Looks proved crucial. On 9 November, 1960, Kennedy squeaked into the White House with a narrow majority, with his pregnant wife Jackie by his side.

U-2 and the shoe

Meanwhile Elvis Presley left the army, American Bandstand host Dick Clark and DJ Alan Freed were accused of involvement in payola, Brian Hyland sang *Itsy Bitsy Teenie Weenie Yellow Polkadot Bikini*, Blacks sat in at "whites only" lunch counters in North Carolina, Alabama and Tennessee. They were gunned down in Sharpeville by South African police. Francis Chichester sailed the Atlantic single-handed. The downing of a U-2 spy plane piloted by American Gary Powers halted a summit conference. Later Soviet premier Nikita Khrushchev interrupted proceedings at the United Nations by taking his shoe off and banging it on the desk.

France revalued the franc, tested its first atomic bomb in the Sahara and saw more trouble in Algeria. Britain gave independence to Cyprus. Belgium did the same for the Congo, only to spark a bloody civil war when the copper-rich province of Katanga seceded. Mao Tse-tung began

1

The two-day summit conference in Vienna between Khrushchev and Kennedy did nothing to ease the situation in Berlin which had been divided by the Wall a month later and seen a 16-hour confrontation between Soviet and American tanks. The Minuteman, America's first three-stage Inter-continental Ballistic Missile, was tested successfully. Now both of the superpowers were in a position to annihilate each other – along with the rest of the northern hemisphere.

Racial politics on the agenda
Student volunteers, both black and white, travelled across the American South in an effort to desegregate inter-state bussing. These Freedom Riders were attacked in Montgomery, Alabama, and martial law was imposed. Bob Dylan played Greenwich Village while uptown the

1 London's Carnaby Street was at the centre of fashionable happenings. It was the place to see and be seen.

spreading his ideas to the masses via his "little red book", which was eventually to become a bible for disaffected Western youth. Doctors developed the artificial kidney, ultramodern Brasilia became the purpose-built capital of Brazil, more Dead Sea scrolls were discovered, Castro nationalized all American property in Cuba and Nazi war criminal Adolf Eichmann was discovered living under a false name in Argentina. And after extensive testing in Puerto Rico, the American Food and Drug Administration approved the sale of an oral contraceptive – the Pill. It was to go on sale the following spring at $10 for a month's supply and would start a sexual revolution.

First into space
1961 began with the newly inaugurated President Kennedy saying that the "torch had been passed to a new generation of Americans" who were exhorted to "ask not what your country can do for you – ask what you can do for your country". Eleven days later America sent the first chimp into space. In April, the Russians won the race to put a man into space when 27-year-old Yuri Gagarin orbited the Earth in a Vostok spacecraft. America countered the Russian response with two 15-minute space hops, the first by Alan Shepard. By August, the Russians had orbited the earth 17 times in a manned shot lasting over 25 hours.

On the ground, President Kennedy visited France with Jackie, launched the abortive Bay of Pigs attack on Cuba, started the Peace Corps and increased the number of military "advisors" in Laos and Vietnam, where the first US soldier, James Davis, had been killed by the Viet Cong.

2 Bob Dylan was the poet of the sixties. Although no one could understand quite what his lyrics meant, they were the perennial topic of conversation for pseudo-intellectuals everywhere. Here he arrives in London for his first British tour in 1965, before he turned from acoustic guitar to electric.

2

3

3 Sir Allen Lane, the founder of Penguin Books, oversaw the publishing revolution of the sixties which – after a heated trial – brought D. H. Lawrence's "obscene" novel Lady Chatterley's Lover *to the bookshelves and opened the floodgates to many previously banned books.*

4 Martin Luther King's programme of non-violent action forced white America to recognize the rights of blacks by sheer weight of moral argument. Gunned down in Memphis on 4 April 1968, he never lived to see his dream come true.

4

swells in the Peppermint Lounge were learning the Twist with Chubby Checker – not to mention the Pony, the Jerk and the Frug. It was even rumoured that they were doing the Twist in the Rose Garden at the White House.

Ernest Hemingway shot himself. *Catch 22* was published – along with Henry Miller's erotic classic *Tropic of Cancer* which had been banned in America since it was written in 1934. James Baldwin came to prominence with *Nobody Knows My Name*. Robert Heinlein wrote *Stranger in a Strange Land* and Irving Stone wrote *The Agony and the Ecstasy*. The silver screen saw *Breakfast at Tiffany's, West Side Story,* Paul Newman in *The Hustler* and *The Guns of Navarone*. Scientists discovered continental drift. South Africa seceded from the British Commonwealth and was condemned by the UN for its racial policies in South-West Africa (now Namibia). In Israel, Adolf Eichmann went on trial for war crimes. He was hanged the next year.

By 1962, Jackie Kennedy had become the queen of Washington, taking the TV cameras on a guided tour of the White House. Meanwhile charismatic Jack had the Cuban missile crisis to tackle. For seven days, the world stood on the brink of a nuclear war. On 22 October, Kennedy showed aerial photographs of missile installations on Cuba, less than 200 miles from the coast of Florida. The US Navy blockaded Cuba. The President threatened retaliation against the Soviet Union if missiles were launched from Cuba. Khrushchev threatened retaliation against the USA for the blockade. A Soviet ship was seen steaming for Cuba. The world held its breath.

Then news came through that the Soviet vessel had changed course and Khrushchev agreed to stop sending missiles if the USA would end its blockade. But the crisis was by no means over. On 26 October intelligence reports showed that work on the missile sites had speeded up in a rush to make them operational. A U-2 spy plane went missing over Cuba and other US aircraft were fired on. Fourteen thousand USAF reservists were called up. Only then did Khrushchev offer to dismantle the missile sites if America withdrew its bases in Turkey. On 28 October, an agreement to that effect was signed. Nuclear holocaust

had been averted by a hair's breadth.

For the Americans, tension ran high at home too. Martin Luther King was in jail in Georgia but released to avoid mass demonstrations. The US government went to the Federal Courts to force school integration and rioting erupted after the first Black, James Meredith, was enrolled at the all-white University of Mississippi after Jack Kennedy had federalized the Mississippi National Guard.

Birth of a legend

Marilyn Monroe was found dead at her home, the victim of a lethal combination of booze and barbituates. Richard Nixon was defeated in his bid to become governor of California and told the press: "You won't have Nixon to kick around any more."

John Glenn became the first American to orbit the Earth. The spacecraft Mariner sent back the first close up pictures of Venus. The Soviets sent a spacecraft to Mars.

And the first communications satellite, Telstar, bounced TV pictures from France and Britain to the US. Eighteen-year-old Peter Fechter became the first person to be killed climbing the Berlin Wall.

Ken Kesey published *One Flew Over the Cuckoo's Nest*. Anthony Burgess contributed *A Clockwork Orange*. James Baldwin wrote *Another Country*. Cartoonist Charles M. Schulz produced *Happiness is a Warm Puppy* featuring a beagle called Snoopy. Rachel Carson published *Silent Spring* while Vladimir Nabokov's controversial novel *Lolita* was filmed by Stanley Kubrick. Pat Boone gave the world *Speedy Gonzales* and four Liverpool lads gave up the grease and had their hair cut in a new and distinctive pudding-basin style.

After giving Algeria its independence, French President Charles de Gaulle narrowly escaped several assassination attempts by the Secret Army Organization – the OAS.

Britain barred from Europe

In 1963, French sports shirt manufacturer René Lacoste patented the metal tennis racket. But his countrymen vetoed Britain's entry to the European Common Market. Scandal rocked the British government when it was discovered that Secretary of War John Profumo was sleeping with a prostitute who was also seeing a lot of a Soviet diplomat. More than £2 million in cash and jewellery was stolen in the Great Train Robbery. Former diplomat Kim Philby, revealed as the third man in the Burgess-Maclean spy ring, escaped to Moscow. The British Secret Service was vindicated though, when James Bond took to the screen in *Dr No*. And it was 1963 which saw the rise in England of the Beatles, the Rolling Stones, the Searchers, Gerry and the Pacemakers and the rest of the Mersey Beat. The Beatles alone had three number one hits in Britain with *From Me To You, She Loves You* and *I Want To Hold Your Hand*.

Alabama Governor George Wallace stood guard at the door of the University of Alabama to prevent two black students enrolling. He was pushed aside. Earlier Kennedy had sent Federal troops into Birmingham to quell riots. Non-violent black leader Martin Luther King told more than 200,000 civil rights demonstrators in Washington: "I have a dream…"

1 Disgraced British Minister of War John Profumo was caught sleeping with prostitute Christine Keeler, who was also sleeping with a Soviet naval attaché. The scandal almost brought down the Conservative government in Britain in 1963.

2 In 1964 fast talking Olympic medal winner Cassius Clay shocked the world when his "float like a butterfly, sting like a bee" style reduced convicted killer Sonny Liston to tears.

3 Cassius Clay – now Muhammad Ali, and a Muslim – confirmed that he was worthy of the world heavy-weight title when he destroyed Floyd Patterson in 1965. He attributed his victory to the "righteous life".

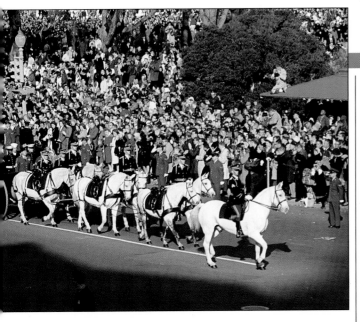

However a new more militant voice was already being heard throughout America. It was that of Malcolm X, a Black Muslim who preached the need for direct action and a separate Black state. Another Muslim leader, the Ayatollah Khomeini was arrested in anti-Shah rioting in Tehran. Three unveiled women were killed by rioters. Meanwhile the Russians put the first woman in space. In Saigon, a Buddhist monk publicly burnt himself to death.

A citizen of Berlin

Kennedy visited the Berlin Wall and said: "Ich bin ein Berliner." (Khrushchev had been to the Wall earlier in the year.) Despite the hardline tone of Kennedy's Berlin speech, a hot-line was opened between Washington and Moscow and the first test-ban treaty was signed. Six weeks later, on 22 November, President Kennedy was assassinated in Dallas. His alleged killer, Lee Harvey Oswald, was himself murdered two days later by club-owner Jack Ruby on live TV. Kennedy was buried in Arlington cemetery. Lyndon Baines Johnson was sworn in as the 36th President of the United States. Jack Ruby was sentenced to death the next year.

It could have all come unravelled then, but the dent in the decade's all-pervasive mood of optimism caused by the death of Kennedy did not last long. The Beatles were coming. *She Loves You* reached number three in the US charts in early December. Two months later, in February 1964, the moptops – followed by the Rolling Stones later in the year and seemingly every other British kid who could carry a guitar – invaded America.

Cassius Clay, later to take the name Muhammad Ali, KOed Sonny Liston to become world heavyweight champion. His secret was simple. He floated like a butterfly, stung like a bee. The temple at Egypt's Abu Simbel was moved to make way for the Aswan Dam and the Supremes had their first hit with *Where Did Our Love Go?* The UN warned that the world was in the throes of a population explosion. Peter Sellers made his first appearance as the incompetent Inspector Clouseau in *The Pink Panther*. The Warren commission investigating Kennedy's assassination found that Lee Harvey Oswald had acted alone. Julie Andrews became Mary Poppins and the Chinese exploded their first atomic bomb.

The pursuit of peace

The Beachboys were getting around while the Animals relaxed in *The House of the Rising Sun*. Martin Luther King won the Nobel Peace Prize. In the American South though, three civil rights activists were murdered, while in the North the first race riots broke out.

LBJ signed into law the Civil Rights Act and a $947.5 million anti-poverty bill. In exchange, he won the Presidential election struggle with Barry Goldwater and Congress passed the Gulf of Tonkin resolution giving the President the right to make war on North Vietnam. In the South, things were hotting up. That year, 136 Americans died in Vietnam. And the US Surgeon General published a report linking smoking to lung cancer.

1965 saw the death at the age of 91 of Churchill and his state funeral. LBJ inaugurated "The Great Society", in

4 *On 25 November 1963, the youngest and most loved president John F. Kennedy was buried at Arlington Cemetery, across the river from the Capitol in Virginia. Having been in office for just a thousand days, much of what he promised had been left undone. President Johnson was left to pursue his policies – giving civil rights to the blacks, welfare to the poor and escalating the war in Vietnam.*

5 *The sixties also saw the old world pass away. On 24 January 1965, Sir Winston Churchill died. He was given a full state funeral.*

which poverty would be outlawed, and sent the Marines into Vietnam. By the end of the year there were 108,000 American troops in 'Nam. Napalm was used for the first time and draft cards were being burnt at home. Meanwhile revolutionary hero Che Guevara set off to incite revolution in Bolivia, where he would be killed two years later.

LBJ announced new anti-poverty measures worth $101 million and signed the Medicare Social Security bill, and – in response to the civil rights march from Selma to Montgomery – introduced the Voting Rights Act. This was seen by many American Blacks as too little, too late. Race riots raged in the Los Angeles ghetto of Watts. Malcolm X was shot dead, following his split from the Black Muslims. In Rhodesia, Prime Minister Ian Smith used UDI – the unilateral declaration of independence – to prevent Black majority rule.

Dylan plugs in

Anthony Quinn became *Zorba the Greek*. Julie Andrews sang *The Sound of Music*. Bob Dylan went electric to the dismay of some of his fans. His girlfriend, Joan Baez, made the charts with *It's All Over Now Baby Blue*. The Who sang: "I hope I die before I get old." The Beatles needed *Help!* The Byrds were *Eight Miles High,* while the Shangri-Las

mourned *The Leader of the Pack*. In space, the Russians – shortly followed by the Americans – went for the first extraterrestrial walk. Two Gemini spacecraft rendezvoused aloft, while on the ground, Americans were seeing UFOs in large numbers.

The following year, 1966, saw two capsules docking in space, though one had to make an emergency landing afterwards. Ralph Nader began his crusade against the automobile industry, declaring that many cars were *Unsafe at Any Speed*. The artificial heart pump was developed. Mao started the cultural revolution in China. In Vietnam, American dead outnumbered Vietnamese for the first time. Protest grew over the continuing conflict. LSD guru Timothy Leary – the Harvard professor who instructed his students to "turn on, tune in and drop out" – was busted for drugs. An American plane lost an H-bomb off the coast of Spain.

Queen Elizabeth II opened Parliament on TV for the first time and Mrs Gandhi became India's prime minister. Maybe it wasn't, as James Brown claimed that year, *A Man's, Man's, Man's World*.

Reagan hits the trail

James Meredith, the first black student at "Ole Miss", was shot during a civil rights march. The streets of Chicago, Cleveland and New York saw race riots and black protesters faced bayonets in Chicago. The first black senator was elected. Florence was flooded. Ronald Reagan was elected governor of California. Across the Atlantic, lone yachtsman Francis Chichester set off on a solo voyage around the world and Twiggy caused a furore by stepping

1 Movie actor Ronald Reagan turned Republican during the sixties – and became governor of California in 1966. By the next year he was urging the use of nuclear weapons against the Viet Cong. Having failed to win the presidential nomination in 1968, he advised that "anarchists and fascists" – that is, peace protesters – should be kicked off campus.

2 In the Six Day War, Israel won a decisive victory over its Arab neighbours. Routing its enemies, Israel reunited Jerusalem under its own control. Victorious Defence Minister Moshe Dayan told his troops at the Wailing Wall: "We have returned to the holiest of our holy places, never to depart from it again."

1

2

off a plane in America wearing a mini-skirt.

Truman Capote penned *In Cold Blood* and Jacqueline Susann *Valley of the Dolls.* Michael Caine played *Alfie,* Paul Scofield *A Man for All Seasons,* Lynn Redgrave *Georgy Girl* and her sister Vanessa the estranged wife of *Morgan – A Suitable Case for Treatment* (David Warner). Raquel Welch set off on her *Fantastic Voyage* while Richard Burton and Elizabeth Taylor showed they weren't afraid of Virginia Woolf. Phil Spector ended his record-producing career when his UK hit, Ike and Tina Turner's *River Deep, Mountain High,* flopped in the States. Nancy Sinatra's boots were made for walking while her father married Mia Farrow and the Beatles sailed away in their *Yellow Submarine.*

With 1967 came the Summer of Love. It brought Be-Ins to New York. The Flowerpot Men suggested: *"Let's All Go To San Francisco."* The Beatles released *Sergeant Pepper's Lonely Hearts Club Band.* Carnaby Street was awash with love beads, bells and kaftans. Jimi Hendrix and the Who appeared at the Monterey pop festival. Elvis married Priscilla. The guru of the New Journalism, Tom Wolfe, took the *Electric Kool-Aid Acid Test.* Anti-war protests broke out across America. Norman Mailer was arrested. Muhammad Ali was stripped of his World Heavyweight boxing title for dodging the draft. Martin Luther King turned against the war. And the head of the US Food and Drug Administration said that the effects of marijuana were no worse than those of alcohol, and called for the decriminalization of the drug.

Shadows over the Summer of Love

Hateful things were happening too, of course. American involvement in the war in Vietnam escalated – backed by Governor Reagan, who urged the use of the Bomb. The colonels seized power in Greece. The Israelis ousted the Arabs in the Six Day War. The province of Biafra seceded from Nigeria, sparking civil war. Three astronauts were burnt to death on the launchpad at Cape Kennedy. De Gaulle called for a free (French) Quebec. A giant oil tanker, the *Torrey Canyon,* split apart off the coast of Cornwall, spilling its cargo and helping to spark the environmental movement.

Race riots ripped through cities large and small – Detroit, New York, Toledo, Ohio, and Grand Rapids, Michigan. Stokely Carmichael and H. Rapp Brown of the Student Non-Violent Co-ordinating Committee called for an armed revolution by the black community. They also pushed for the use of "Black" instead of "Negro". Meanwhile Thurgood Marshall became the first Black to be appointed to the Supreme Court and Sidney Poitier faced down a racist Rod Steiger *In The Heat of the Night.*

The Beatles' manager Brian Epstein died. Batman biffed it out on TV. Britain withdrew from Aden. The British pound was devalued. The House of Lords lost its legislative powers. Jim Morrison of the Doors called on fans to *Light My Fire.* The Boston strangler was arrested after killing 13 women. Dr Christiaan Barnard performed

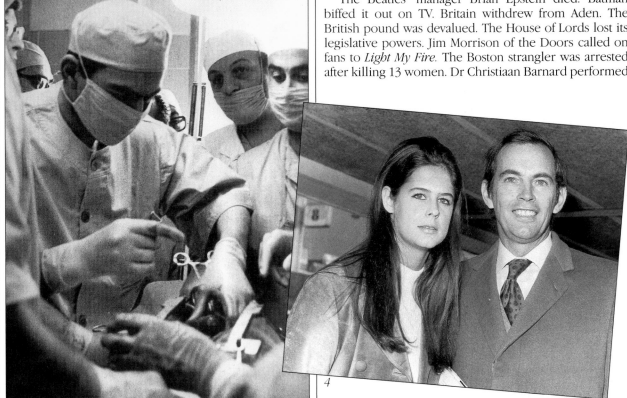

3

4

3 South African surgeon Dr Christiaan Barnard performed the first human heart transplant in December 1969. The patient, Louis Washkansky, lived 18 days. Here Dr Barnard demonstrates his method of heart transplant on a dog in Madrid, Spain. The dog, a stray, died after the operation.

4 Christiaan Barnard finished the sixties by writing a book, One Life, and marrying a 19-year-old. His European honeymoon doubled as a book-promotion tour.

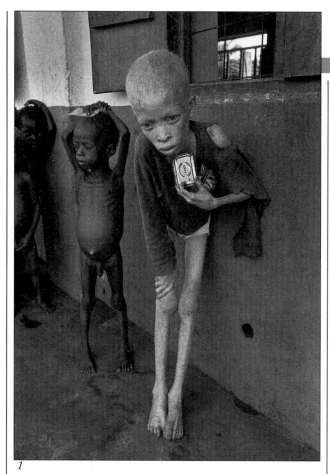

1

the first heart transplant. Concorde was rolled out. The first microwave oven was unveiled. Jane Fonda was *Barbarella*. Dustin Hoffman was *The Graduate*. Warren Beatty and Faye Dunaway were *Bonnie and Clyde*. And Katharine Hepburn asked Spencer Tracy *Guess Who's Coming to Dinner?*

The year of lost illusions

1968 was the year it all came apart. The Tet offensive brought Viet Cong soldiers into the American Embassy compound – live on TV screens around the world – showing the American people for the first time that the war was unwinnable. And the world stood by and watched as Russian tanks rumbled into Czechoslovakia to crush the attempted liberalization of communism known as the Prague Spring. LBJ announced that he would not run for President again, but came close to civil war when protesters took on Mayor Daley's police outside the Democratic convention in Chicago. Starvation swept Biafra. France was paralysed in May by strikes lead by students under revolutionary Danny Cohn-Bendit. An El Al jet was hijacked to Algiers.

Martin Luther King was assassinated by James Earl Ray. Race riots rocked Chicago, Baltimore, Washington and Cincinnati, and the clenched-fist of the Black Power salute was seen at the Mexico Olympics. Black Panther leader Huey Newton was convicted of murder. Eldridge Cleaver

put his *Soul On Ice*. Standing as an anti-war candidate in the primaries, Bobby Kennedy was shot and killed by Sirhan Sirhan. Pop artist Andy Warhol was shot by Valerie Solanis of SCUM – the Society for Cutting Up Men. And Richard Nixon won the Presidential election this time. Little consolation could be drawn from the halt of bombing of North Vietnam and the opening of the Paris Peace talks, the Beatles visit to the Maharishi and the marriage of Jackie Kennedy to Greek shipping tycoon Aristotle Onassis.

A giant step for mankind

The year 1969 was a fitting culmination to the sixties. Neil Armstrong and Buzz Aldrin stepped into a new era when they walked on the moon. Ho Chi Minh – the father of Vietnam – died. President de Gaulle fell from power, Richard Nixon was elevated to it and began troop withdrawals from Vietnam. A quarter of a million peace protesters converged on Washington. Anti-war activists seized college campuses and Black militants took over Cornell University. Eldridge Cleaver fled to Algeria, Stokely Carmichael to Guinea. Black Panther Bobby Seale was arrested for murder. Timothy Leary was cleared of drug charges in the Supreme Court. British troops withdrew from east of Suez but moved into Northern Ireland. Britain banned capital punishment.

That year, nearly half a million people congregated at Woodstock to hear the sixties rock. Yasser Arafat came to prominence and Colonel Gaddafi seized power in Libya. Alexander Solzhenitsyn was expelled from the Soviet writers' union. The Weathermen terrorist group began their bombing campaign in American cities. Lieutenant William Calley was arrested for the murder of 567 Vietnamese civilians at Mylai. Actress Sharon Tate – wife of film director Roman Polanski – and four others were murdered by Charles Manson's "Family". Marvin Gaye *Heard It Through The Grapevine*. The Rolling Stones extolled *Honky Tonk Women*. Credence Clearwater Revival sensed there was a *Bad Moon Rising*. John Lennon and the Plastic Ono Band naïvely asked us to *Give Peace a Chance*. Four months into 1970, the Beatles finally broke up.

Aquarius waning

Easy Rider took to the screen, *Hair* to the stage – though, in retrospect, it seems to have been the end of the *Age of Aquarius* rather than the beginning. Philip Roth wrote *Portnoy's Complaint,* Kurt Vonnegut *Slaughterhouse Five,* Mario Puzo *The Godfather*. Paul Newman and Robert Redford starred in *Butch Cassidy and the Sundance Kid,* Steve McQueen in *Bullitt,* Dustin Hoffman in *Midnight Cowboy*. The disillusionment was complete.

It has been said that those who can remember the sixties weren't really there. But for those who can recall

1 Vietnam was not the only war of the sixties. More pitiful still was the war in Biafra. On 30 May, 1967, the eastern province of Nigeria seceded and proclaimed itself the independent state of Biafra. Though the rebel forces put up stiff resistance, the Nigerian federal government in Lagos managed to starve the secessionists into submission in 1970 – at a predictably high cost.

those years, 1970 seems to mark the end of a golden age. America's inability to extricate itself from the Vietnam war, the termination of the Great Society welfare programmes, the oil crisis sparked by the Six Day War, the cynicism and greed of the pop music industry, the ever-lengthening list of drug casualties, the winding-down of the space programme, the collapse of the New Left and the failure of the "youth revolution" left even the young bitter and rudderless.

However, the sixties had at last succeeded in throwing off the heavy legacy of World War II. They laid the foundations for many of the movements which are with us today – women's and gay liberation, the quest for racial integration, concern with the environment – and, of course, consumerism. The sixties also established a new freedom of expression and social interaction that have not, yet, been reversed. Concorde and the Jumbo jet took to the air and the first desktop computer was unveiled. And though younger generations now view much of what went on in the sixties as silly and self-indulgent, for those who lived through that time, it was a glorious spring in which to be alive.

3 In May 1968, the revolution seemed to be at hand. Across the western world, student protest erupted. In France, they closed the Sorbonne for the first time in its 700-year history and sparked a general strike which almost toppled President de Gaulle. In response, the government threatened to use force to prevent the take-over of a "Communist dictatorship".

2

2 Vice President in the fifties, Nixon was defeated in the presidential race by John F. Kennedy in 1960, largely because of his poor showing on TV. In 1962, Nixon failed to get elected as Governor of California. But in 1968, sold like soap powder, Nixon was back in the White House with a promise to end the war in Vietnam.

3

19

Cambridge History Faculty, James Stirling.

CHAPTER ONE

CONCRETE AND CLAY

"They paved paradise, put up a parking lot."

JONI MITCHELL

CONCRETE AND CLAY

The sixties were a period of fervent architectural activity. European cities were finishing their post-war reconstruction, although making good the damage caused by war was not enough. Planners saw themselves as social engineers out to make a brave new world by demolishing slums and housing the disadvantaged in shining cities in the sky. Burgeoning relatively young countries like Australia and Brazil aimed to steal a march on the old world with costly architectural status symbols. And no emerging Third World country could possibly hold its head high on the world stage without first transforming its ancient capital into a glistening imitation of downtown Chicago. The International Style was everywhere to be seen.

The fruits of Modernism

Developed in Europe by Le Corbusier, Walter Gropius, Mies van der Rohe and others, the International Style found fertile soil in America, to which many of its instigators fled in the 1930s to escape persecution and imminent war. In the forties and fifties they began to put their ideas into practice and, in the 1960s, the downtown area of practically every city in the eastern United States was rebuilt in the Modernist genre.

Hundreds of new architectural firms sprung up. Established practices employed staffs numbering in the hundreds. And, in Britain especially, young architects found themselves in charge of major urban projects.

With the creation of Brasilia as Brazil's new capital in 1960, the world saw the birth of the first Modernist city. A new age seemed to be dawning. Urban centres were all set to be transformed into earthly paradises. By the end of the decade, though, that dream – like many of the buildings it inspired – lay in ruins. The vast Pruitt-Igoe workers' housing project in St Louis designed by Minoru Yamasaki, for example, had to be dynamited in 1972 – at the residents' request! And in 1968 the factory-made high-rise Ronan Point in London's East End collapsed like a pack of cards after a minor gas explosion. It had been completed just two years earlier.

1 Brasilia was the most daring experiment in city planning of the sixties. Brazil cleared the jungle to build itself a new capital on fixed Corbusian principles. This is the Palace of Justice designed by Oscar Niemeyer.

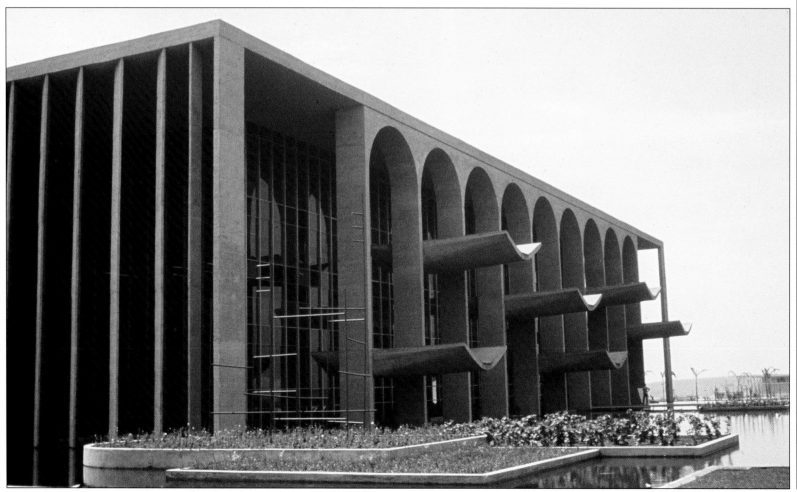

Elsewhere, areas between the tower blocks designated for social interaction became arid, windswept wastelands. Rough concrete surfaces became the perfect canvas for spray-can graffiti artists. Le Corbusier's "streets in the sky" became public toilets and the haunt of muggers and dope dealers. Older residents found they could not adapt their ways to fit in with the planners' dreams. The young became angry or alienated. Anyone who could afford it, quit the new Utopia.

An experiment under attack

Not just the residents but the public in general began to protest that whole areas of their cities were being demolished to make way for what they now saw as a failed social experiment. Eventually the planners were forced to put away their designs for windy walkways, gleaming towers, instant space-age cities. Even architects became disillusioned. Oscar Neuman questioned, in his *Defensible Space*, the whole 1930s idealistic concept of communal living, with its large park areas that no one identified with, while Jane Jacobs attacked the Modernists' arrogant rejection of traditional street patterns and established ways of life in *The Death and Life of Great American Cities*.

Even in the early sixties, some attempt had been made to restrain the excesses of Modernism. In Britain, James Stirling began to temper the Modernist approach with more traditional ideas. His engineering block at Leicester University – designed with James Gowan – used glass and steel, along with the engineering brick of the Victorian era. In America, Edward Durrell Stone began to use curved lines, marble and decoration in buildings such as his Huntington Hartford Gallery of Modern Art and his Kennedy Center in Washington. Minoru Yamasaki rediscovered the Gothic arch in his Science Pavilion at Seattle's 1962 World Fair. This was to be repeated later in his work on the entrance-ways to the twin towers of New York's World Trade Center.

Mix-and-match architecture

The theorist of this new departure was Robert Venturi, who wrote *Complexity and Contradiction in Architecture* in 1966 and, later, *A Significance for A&P Parking Lots, or Learning from Las Vegas*. He argued that the Modernists' humourless functionalism belonged to the grey days of the thirties. In the hedonistic spirit of the sixties, Mies van der Rohe's "less is more" had become "less is bore". Venturi urged architects to borrow from other styles they saw around them, even from the shameless pop-art heaven of Las Vegas. But, like so many of the architectural theorists who had gone before him, he did not complete many buildings.

Early in his career, Venturi had worked with Eero Saarinen and Louis Kahn. Saarinen had already turned

2

Modernism on its head with his design for the TWA terminal at what was then Idlewild – now Kennedy – Airport. Completed in 1962, it was built in conventional materials – concrete, glass, steel – but it was shaped like an eagle in flight. Perhaps even more ambitious was his terminal building at Washington DC's Dulles Airport which resembles a wing ready for take-off.

When Saarinen died in 1961, his practice was taken over by Paul Rudolph who went on to design the Boston Government Services Center and the architectural faculty at Yale. Louis Kahn built the blank-faced extension to the Yale University Art Gallery and, in 1962, began work on Bangladesh's National Assembly Building in Dacca, with its concentration on heavy geometric forms. These men, along with the later work of Le Corbusier, pioneered Brutalism, which treated buildings more as expressionistic sculptures than as, in Le Corbusier's earlier concept, machines for living or working in.

In England, Denys Lasdun contributed the National Theatre in London. This building was designed to be read as a series of geological strata. But its box-cast concrete has not weathered well, leaving it with the bleak, grey walls of a prison.

An Olympian feat

In Japan, Kenzo Tange used sweeping sculptured concrete forms for his Kagawa Prefectural Centre. And for the 1964 Tokyo Olympics, he enclosed two arenas in

2 Denys Lasdun pushed the Modernist movement in the direction of New Brutalism. His uncompromising National Theatre in London's South Bank arts complex is intended to be read as a series of geological strata.

1

massive tents of steel plates the swirling roofs of which were supported by concrete masts and massive steel cables. But perhaps the most successful – at least, the best-known and liked – of the buildings created in this sculptural style is the Sydney Opera House. Designed in 1957, it was not completed until 1973 – long after the architect Jorn Utzon, a Danish pupil of Aalto's, had quit the project. Its costs overran disastrously and its modified design is far from perfect for staging opera. But in spite of its troubled history the great shell-like roofs of the opera house, which seem to echo the billowing sails of the yachts in the harbour it dominates, have made it the new symbol of that city.

The great showcase for innovative architecture at the height of the sixties was Expo '67 in Montreal. The long-time guru of Modernism, Buckminster Fuller, built a massive geodesic dome there. This light-weight system-built structure soon became a watchword of hippy culture. But the geodesic dome did not go on to provide the low-cost housing many Utopians had hoped for. Instead it was used extensively by the US Defense Department to house its early-warning radar system.

Problems in practice

One of the other eye-catching experiments at Expo '67 was Moshe Safdie's Habitat. This used production-line techniques to produce – not the straight up and down of the housing project high rise – but a higgledy-piggledy stack of human-scale housing units. Unfortunately, this bold experiment failed. Complete standardization of components was not possible as the units at the bottom of the building had to be strong enough to support those above. Traditional site-built, timber-framed houses would have been cheaper to construct. And when other Habitat-style buildings were constructed for longer-term use, they soon showed all the disadvantages of their by-now traditional high-rise, system-built cousins – leaking joints, condensation, and ill-fitting doors and windows.

1 Never a mainstream Modernist, the architect and theorist Richard Buckminster Fuller was a revolutionary who blazed the trail with new material and new forms. His huge geodesic dome which was the United States Pavilion at Expo '67 in Montreal was widely praised. But, ironically, the only practical use for this sort of structure was by the US military, to house its early-warning radar system.

Some architects – like the Dutchman John Habraken, the Belgian Lucien Kroll and the former student of Frank Lloyd Wright, Paoli Soleri, in America – rejected the architect's traditional role and sought to be more responsive to the community, to the people who actually lived in their constructions. Habraken wrote *Supports: an alternative to mass housing,* in which he argued that mass housing should be flexible enough for individuals to tailor their homes to their own needs. However his ideas surfaced only in a few experimental estates in London. Kroll built the medical students' hall of residence at Louvain University in Belgium. The students were allowed to design their own rooms and Kroll devised a system of flexible partitions which allowed future occupants to make changes that suited them. The builders were also encouraged to make a contribution to the design and the façade ended up like a giant collage of different styles and materials.

Soleri went even further. He dropped out of society completely and established a commune in the Arizona desert where those who shared his concept of the future would pay to participate in his visionary work. Although his output was not large, his drawings inspired many. He became the role model for "alternative" builders and was influential with a new generation of community architects who hired themselves out to tenants' groups.

Putting function first

There was no shortage of off-the-wall ideas in the sixties, especially in Britain. In 1965, the design theorist Reyner Banham came up with the Unhouse. Deeply influenced by Buckminster Fuller's technological ideas and the massive – one could almost say architectural – constructions of the space industry, Banham believed that the construction of the services needed in a modern house – the air-conditioning, the plumbing, the central heating, the wiring – could make it possible to do away with the "house" altogether.

Cedric Price was another visionary. The designer of the huge aviary that dominates London Zoo, he came up with such novel ideas as the transportable weekend home and spent much of the sixties working on designs for a giant Fun Palace.

The magazine *Archigram* also threw away functionalism in favour of fun. The *Archigram* team – Peter Cook, Warren Chalk, Dennis Crompton, David Greene, Ron Herron and Mike Webb – produced plans for Plug-In Cities, Fun Cities, Walking Cities and futuristic projects. Many of their notions were much influenced by science fiction, which Pop Art had made into a vogue at the time. They extolled expendability and saw some of their ideas put into practice in the giant inflatables used at outdoor pop festivals. Although the *Archigram* group did not actually build anything, its influence has been far reaching,

2

and can be seen these days in everything from the Portakabin to the Pompidou Centre in Paris.

Symbols of masculinity

While the young architects were having fun and planning their great vision of the future, the giant multinational corporations continued to feel the need to express their power and masculine self-confidence in giant skyscrapers. These were provided by, among others, Philip Johnson and Gordon Bunshaft, who oversaw work at the world's biggest architectural firm, Skidmore, Owings & Merrill. In 1970, Bruce Graham of SOM fulfilled the Corbusian ideal of mixing apartments, offices and shops over the one hundred floors of the John Hancock Center in Chicago. He went on to produce the 110-floor Sears Tower, the world's tallest building.

Even swinging London was not immune from this onrush of corporate identity. In 1965, the Post Office Tower went up. It became the city's newest landmark. It is an unmistakably phallic symbol of technological progress.

2 In private housing, as well as in public architecture, New Brutalism raised its deliberately ugly head. But in this house, designed in 1969 by the British firm Aldington and Craig, the harshness of the board-marked concrete has been mellowed by the use of a slightly less severe brick in a circular, pseudo-chimney. The architects were determined not to let their client have a bourgeois garden, though.

INSPIRATIONS

1 *The flat monoliths of Stonehenge were much copied in the sixties. Architects seemed to believe that people could get in touch with themselves better if housed in primitive structures. They did: they behaved like cavemen painting on the walls, hunting in packs and ritually sacrificing young maidens and old-aged pensioners.*

2 *Bauhaus was another inspiration, with its idealized view of the "workers" that became so fashionable again in the sixties. The Bauhaus designs romanticized the workers to such a degree that they thought they wanted to live in factories.*

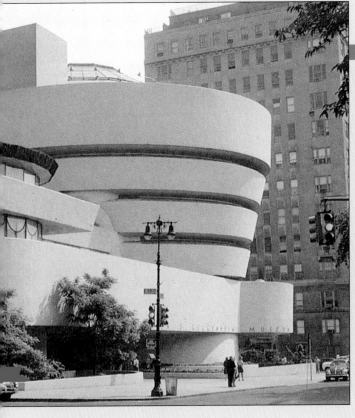

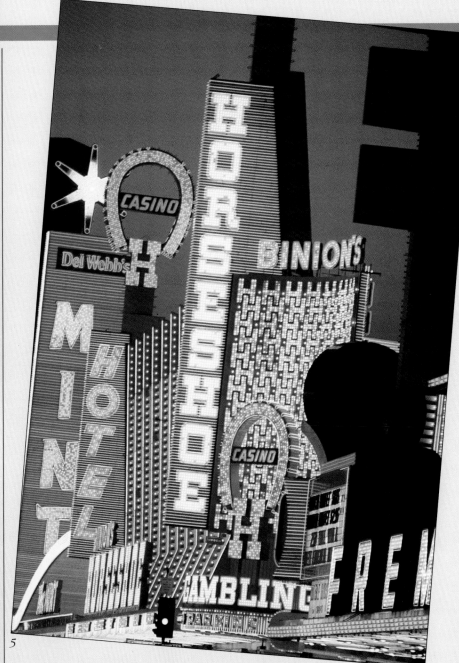

5

3 Le Corbusier was the name on every sixties' architect's lips. He was the great god with his weird theory that architecture was an "explosioration" of form and space and light, as deep and mystical in its way as any religious quest. Designed by Le Corbusier these are the capital buildings in Chandigarh in Punjab state.

4 The native American style of Frank Lloyd Wright began to re-assert itself against the flood tide of the International Style in the sixties. Wright's spiral Guggenheim art gallery proved that a modern building did not have to be austere and boring.

5 The sprawling cities of America's west – built after the invention of the motor car – became the model many planners tried to impose on other, older cities. Robert Venturi laid out the philosophy in black and white in Learning from Las Vegas in 1972.

CORPORATE VIRILITY

1 and 2 Richard Seifert decided that the West End of London needed a new focus. So he built the towering Centre Point at the corner of Oxford Street and Charing Cross Road. The building paid eloquent testimony to the burgeoning property empire of the owner, Harry Hyams, yet most of its offices stood empty for the next twenty years.

3 Cities liked to show off too – and then, as now, they chose to do it in the arts. New York's Lincoln Center, opened in 1966, is the home of the Met. The building was designed by Wallace K. Harrison, its murals were by Marc Chagall.

1

3

2

4

4 Walter Gropius was one of the great heroes of the Bauhaus and the International Movement. But though his Pan Am building in New York flaunts the company's virility, it dwarfed the civilized proportions of Park Avenue and led to doubts about his judgment.

5 Even London's conservative St James's could not resist the advance of New Brutalism. Sir Robert Matthew's New Zealand House in Pall Mall uses the Le Corbusian device of placing raised slabs on a podium.

6 London's Post Office Tower is the most unashamedly phallic of buildings. Designed during Harold Wilson's "white heat of the technological revolution", it was the Post Office's new microwave communications centre and consciously gave the organization a new image. The old "penny post" had come into the 21st Century.

5

6

SCULPTURAL STYLE

1 *Denys Lasdun intended his much-derided National Theatre to be read as a series of geological strata. Its board-marked concrete has not weathered well and country-house traditionalists criticize it as one of the worst examples of the New Brutalism. Others see it as a worthy neighbour of the Royal Festival Hall and the Hayward Gallery, confidently completing London's South Bank arts complex.*

2 *James Stirling's History Faculty at Cambridge University, completed in 1966. Its sculptural use of glass contrasts with the use of glazed engineering brick in the Victorian industrial tradition – a technique Stirling had employed in the Engineering Faculty building at Leicester University and the Florey building at Queen's College, Oxford.*

3 *The Twin Towers of the World Trade Center in New York were begun in 1962 and completed fifteen years later. Designed by Minoru Yamasaki.*

4 *The School of Art and Architecture of Yale University at New Haven, Connecticut uses a textured surface to much the same effect as in the building above.*

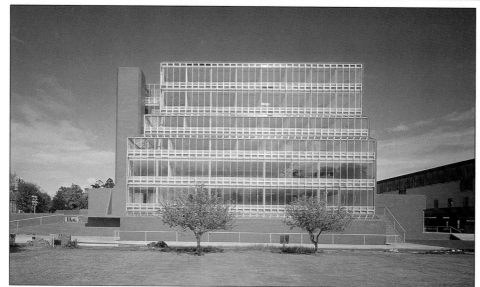

2

3

4

1

5 *John Utzon's troubled design for what turned out to be this extraordinary opera house – with its shell-like roofs echoing the sails of the boats in the harbour – gave Sydney, Australia, a new symbol of the age.*

5

6

6 *The sculptural style applied in the industrial world as well. The Fawley Power Station owes much to the burgeoning space industry.*

7 *The interior of Eero Saarinen's TWA Terminal at New York's Kennedy Airport (1962) shows concrete pillars moulded into sculptural forms.*

8 *The outside of the TWA Terminal, constructed like the wings of a bird, is the real, inspired triumph of the sculptural style.*

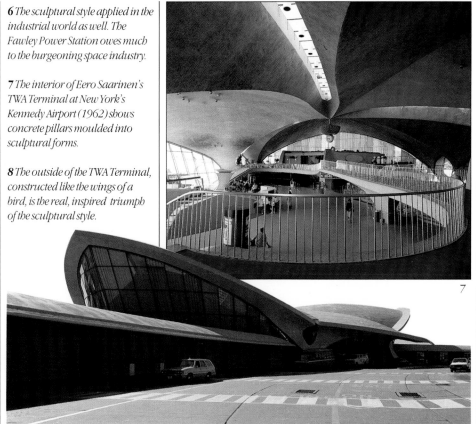

7

8

31

2 *A Corbusian in the pre-war period, Denys Lasdun went on to create some of the seminal works of the sixties in Britain – the Royal College of Physicians in London in 1960, the University of East Anglia in Norwich (shown here) between 1962 and 1968, and the National Theatre on London's South Bank, begun in 1967. These buildings show that he had abandoned the strict utilitarian Modernism of the thirties in favour of a strongly sculptural style.*

3 *Lasdun's campus at Norwich used forms suggested by the landscape and was much copied. Appropriately enough, the University of East Anglia was soon to become one of the hotbeds of sixties student radicalism.*

1 *The Engineering and Science block at the Polytechnic of Central London makes its effect with sheer expanses of board-marked concrete.*

1

2

3

4

4 *James Stirling was one of the many architects who abandoned their allegiance to functionalism in the sixties. This building at St Andrews, in Scotland, lends much to Modernism and blends into its rural surroundings rather than imposing order on them.*

5 *Bertrand Goldberg's Marina City in Chicago – built between 1964 and 1968 – displays an almost organic form. The car-parking floors are separated from the apartments by a service floor.*

6 *Sculpted into the landscape, this house was designed by Richard Rogers and Norman Foster. Even though it melds into the undergrowth, the shape is still strong, dynamic and, above all, modern.*

7 *Frank Lloyd Wright's Marin County Civic Center was built after his death, from 1959 to 1962. Its insistent geometry has a native Spanish inspiration, but the huge scale of the building leaves it sitting on its California hillside like a downed flying saucer. It owes nothing to the International Style that had dominated American architecture since the 1940s.*

5

6

7

HOUSING PROJECTS

1 *There were alternatives to the tower block in cheap welfare housing. Darbourne and Darke tried to create an English version of Le Corbusier's Unité d'Habitation at their housing project in Lillington Street, central London. Built in 1961, it was intended to give welfare housing a picturesque and human face by disguising stark Modernism behind traditional brick and a higgledy-piggledy skyline.*

2 *Many of the architects of the period had their hearts in the right place. Their aim was to sweep away the slums and replace them with modern, functional buildings. They were not just architects – they were social engineers. They believed that the social ills of the ghetto could be solved with proper welfare housing. This example in Harlem seems to have caused as many problems as it solved. Many of the New York housing projects are centres of violent crime, prostitution and "crack" dealing. Elsewhere they have been demolished.*

2

1

3 *The halls of residence at the University of East Anglia, designed by Denys Lasdun, seemed to be exemplary housing in a rural setting, belying the fact that many a student plot was hatched here.*

4 *This building for married students at Cambridge, Massachusetts was designed by Sert Jackson and Gourlay Associates. But it did not keep them off the streets protesting against the Vietnam war.*

3

5 *The interior of Denys Lasdun's halls of residence at the University of East Anglia aimed to give students the privacy to study and socialize. He counted without the sexual and political revolution that was going on at that time.*

6 *Not all the new housing of the period was stark and alienating, as Peter Aldington proved. This is his own award-winning home in Buckinghamshire.*

5

4

6

WILD IDEAS THAT NEVER HAPPENED

1 Although the Archigram group did not produce any buildings, its ideas were influential. Notions of expendability and of architecture as a consumer product turned on a whole generation of younger architects – but outraged their older, more established colleagues. The outrage exploded with the publication, in 1964, of Peter Cook's Plug-in City. Instead of planning for the foreseeable future, it proposed that over a 40-year period outmoded units could be replaced with new, more up-to-date modules.

2 From 1965, Ron Herron and Warren Chalk toyed with the idea of Gasket or Capsule Homes. These Family Cages or Pre-Family dwellings were designed assembled on a custom-made pier.

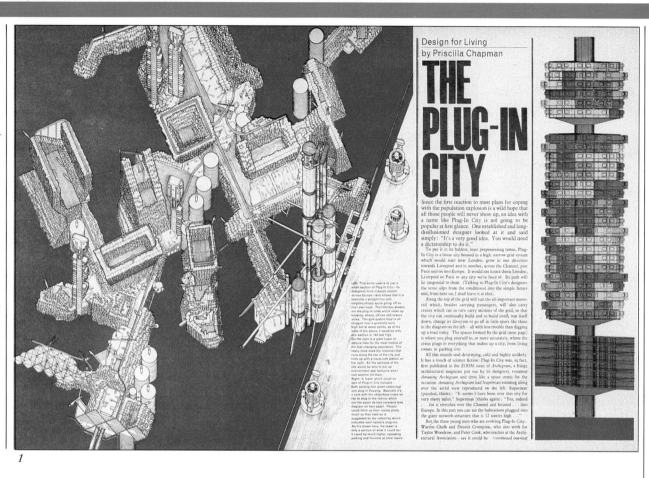

Design for Living
by Priscilla Chapman

THE PLUG-IN CITY

Since the first reaction to most plans for coping with the population explosion is a wild hope that all those people will never show up, an idea with a name like Plug-In City is not going to be popular at first glance. One established and long-disillusioned designer looked at it and said simply: "It's a very good idea. You would need a dictatorship to do it."

To put it in its baldest, least prepossessing terms, Plug-In City is a linear city housed in a high, narrow grid system which would start near London, grow in one direction towards Liverpool and in another, across the Channel, past Paris and on into Europe. It would not knock down London, Liverpool or Paris or any city we're fond of. Its path will lie tangential to them. (Talking to Plug-In City's designers the tense slips from the conditional into the simple future and, from here on, I shall leave it at that.)

Along the top of the grid will run the all-important mono-rail which, besides carrying passengers, will also carry cranes which can in turn carry sections of the grid, so that the city can continually build and re-build itself, tear itself down, change its direction or go off in little spurs like those in the diagram on the left – all with less trouble than digging up a road today. The spaces formed by the grid (next page) is where you plug yourself in, or more accurately, where the crane plugs in everything that makes up a city, from living rooms to parking lots.

All this sounds soul-destroying, cold and highly unlikely. It has a touch of science fiction: Plug-In City was, in fact, first published in the ZOOM issue of Archigram, a fringe architectural magazine put out by its designers, renamed *Amazing Archigram* and done like a space comic for the occasion. *Amazing Archigram* had Superman zooming along over the aerial view reproduced on the left. Superman (puzzled, thinks): "It seems I have been over this city for very many miles." Superman (thinks again): "Yes, indeed . . . for it stretches over the Channel and beyond . . . into Europe. In this part you can see the habitations plugged into the giant network-structure that is 12 stories high . . ."

But the three young men who are evolving Plug-In City – Warren Chalk and Dennis Crompton, who also work for Taylor Woodrow, and Peter Cook, who teaches at the Architectural Association – say it could be *(continued overleaf*

Left: This aerial view is of just a small section of Plug-In City – its designers think it would stretch across Europe – and shows that it is basically a straight line with neighbourhood buns going off on their own hook. The little box-shapes are the plug-in units which make up housing, shops, offices and leisure areas. The grid system they're all slotted into is generally fairly high but at some points, as at the apex of the apex, it could be only one section or 144 feet high.

On the right is a giant tower of serviceless flat for the real mobile of the fast-changing population. The heavy lines mark the monorail that runs along the top of the city and links up with a hovercraft station on the right. All the sections of the city would be able to pull up environment seal balloons when bad weather hit them.

Right: A tower which could be part of Plug-In City includes both parking (the green colouring) and plug-in housing. Basically it's a core with the ubiquitous crane on top to plug in the rotors, which are like super de luxe caravans (see diagram on next page). People could hitch up their rooms pretty much as they liked as is suggested by the colouring which indicates each family's plug-in. As it's drawn here, the tower is only a section of what it could be: it could be much higher, repeating parking and housing at other levels.

1

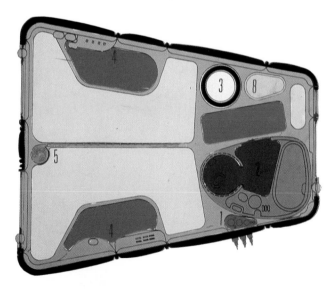

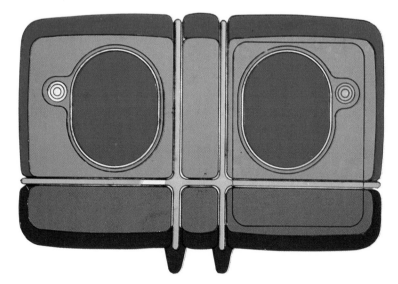

2

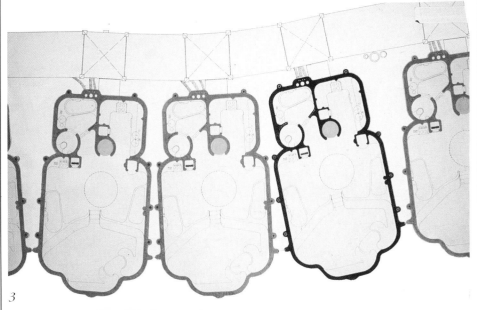

3

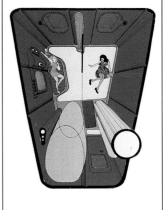

4

3 *Gasket Homes would be factory-made modules, plugged together into communal utilities.*

4 *The capsules would be made simply out of the superimposition of gaskets.*

5 *In 1969, Peter Cook devised the Instant City. Study/Think/Info/Play centres, nightclubs, "light-sound", "responsive" tents, arenas, music domes and car parking could all be assembled "instantly" using balloons.*

5

EXPO '67

1

2

1 Expo '67 in Montreal, Canada, was one of the seminal events of the decade. It was also the great showplace for new architectural ideas. Throughout the sixties, Britain was very much the centre of world attention: "England swings like a pendulum do." Here the British pavilion at Montreal looms over the revolutionary "mini-rail". Maybe it was what was inside that counted, but the innovative use of the Union Jack gave the pavilion a special appeal.

2 The pyramid was considered "cosmic" at the time – but not this way up! The top of the so-called "katimavik" of the Canadian pavilion could be reached by a stairway or elevator. On the left is the "People of Canada" tree. Montreal's Expo '67 was an important event for Canada – as a vital recognition of its own identity rather than just the USA's northern neighbour.

3 *The pavilion of Trinidad and Tobago, and Grenada. These emerging countries were full of ethnic pride – a new sensation for many in the sixties. A steel band performed on the circular platform in the lagoon in front. In the background is the French pavilion.*

3

4 *The spires of the West German pavilion supported a roof of steel net, lined with a 100,000-square-foot (9,300-square-metre) transparent skin. A new generation was coming of age in West Germany, a generation untainted by the Second World War. The soft teepee-style was a deliberate change from the hard, old-style Germany. At the centre of the Cold War, German youth became more radical than other Europeans – and more determined to find a new way ahead.*

5 *The mini-rail crosses one of the many channels where motorized gondolas ply their way. Updating the ancient in this crass fashion was for some one of the most endearing traits of the sixties.*

4

5

Roy Lichtenstein, Whaam! 1965.

CHAPTER TWO

COKE
BOTTLES
AND
CAMPBELL
SOUP CANS

INTRODUCTION

When Emile de Antonio visited successful commercial artist Andy Warhol, Warhol showed him two uncommissioned canvases. One was a picture of a Coke bottle with Abstract-Expressionist hash marks halfway up the side. The other was a plain, stark Coke bottle, outlined in black and white.

De Antonio said: 'One of these is a piece of shit...The other is remarkable.' Warhol destroyed the one with the Abstract-Expressionist hash marks, quit working in advertising and went on to become the most barefaced exponent of Pop Art.

The roots of Pop Art

Although many of the icons of Pop Art are American, the movement actually began in England in 1955 when John McHale returned from a trip to the USA with a trunkful of magazines. Back in austere England, these magazines portrayed America as a promised land of affluence, expendability and built-in obsolescence, the home of technology and up-to-date culture. In 1956 – while American Abstract-Expressionists were still flinging paint at the canvas – McHale, Richard Hamilton, Eduardo Paolozzi and others of the so-called Independent Group used images from these magazines to stage the first Pop Art exhibition in London's Whitechapel Gallery. It was called 'This Is Tomorrow'. Hamilton's work included a robot carrying an unconscious girl superimposed on a film still showing Marilyn Monroe – her first appearance as a Pop icon – and the influential collage 'Just What Is It That Makes Today's Home So Different, So Appealing?' This included images of a modern man and woman, space, cinema, domestic appliances, cars, comics and television, all cut from McHale's magazines. It also included the word "Pop" on the cover of a tennis racket.

But for these early English Pop artists, Pop was something of an intellectual exercise. They were far removed from the images they utilized. The single exception to this rule was Peter Blake, who developed a pop style independently of the Independent Group using British pop stars such as Marty Wilde as icons.

For American Pop Artists though, the images of Pop Art were drawn from the stuff of everyday life. Andy Warhol, for example, simply depicted the objects he knew and loved. He said that he moved on from Coke bottles to Campbell's Soup cans simply because he had a can of that company's soup for lunch every day. And because he had had soup day after day, it seemed reasonable to depict can after can in neat rows.

The art of absence

Even though Warhol's obsession with Campbell's Soup cans sprang from personal experience, there was nothing personal about his treatment of them. His approach is totally depersonalized, presenting them – and other

1 Andy Warhol was the definitive sixties artist. Although he did not invent Pop Art – it came from England – he, more than any other, crystallized its images. A commercial artist by training, Warhol could turn his hand to a flower – one of the most enduring symbols of the decade – as easily as to a Coke bottle.

2 Derek Boshier's The Identi-kit Man. The Identi-kit method of building up a picture of criminal suspect was new in the sixties. This picture, though, uses another Pop image – toothpaste. His paintings often take the form of something else – an envelope, a jigsaw puzzle, a snooker table – but are also informed with something straight out of the headlines: Sharpeville, Gagarin, a 50-Megaton Bomb.

1

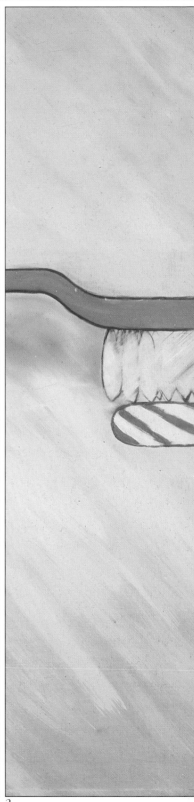

2

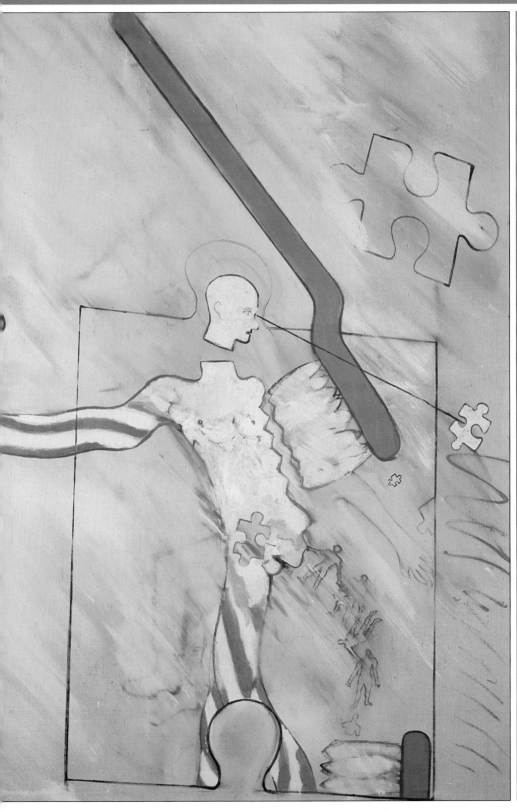

consumer icons – exactly as they are found on the shelves of any supermarket. Soon he even gave up *painting* them at all. Using silk-screen printing, he could depersonalize his images to the point where he did not even have to produce them himself. Sometimes he just stacked cans, or Brillo Pad boxes in an art gallery. Was it sculpture or was it a supermarket?

Warhol revelled in this kind of kitsch. Soup cans, Coke bottles, toothpaste tubes, posters of pop idols and movie stars were the world western man inhabited. Warhol said he could not imagine living in a spiritual nirvana like Nepal or Tibet, or any "tiny, nothing place" in the Himalayas: "I don't ever want to live any place where you couldn't drive down the road and see drive-ins and giant ice-cream cones and walk-in hot dogs and motel signs flashing." That is not to say that his style was uncontrived. Its flat, ultra-realistic treatment was the exact opposite of the aesthetic of the Abstract-Expressionists who, until the birth of Pop, dominated the art world.

Although he was ridiculed at first, it was soon seen that Warhol, in typical sixties style, was simply celebrating the modern world. His images were democratic. Everyone could recognize a soup can. It is his Campbell's Soup can – not, say, one of Jackson Pollock's action paintings – that has become the enduring image of the age.

Warhol went on to produce multiple coloured images of cult figures – Marilyn Monroe, Elvis Presley, Marlon Brando, Elizabeth Taylor, the Mona Lisa, Jackie Kennedy in grief. But in many ways Warhol himself became his greatest work of art. He appeared ordinary, self-effacing, yet almost everything about his image was carefully cultivated. Described by a critic at the time as "a nameless face, as unobtrusive as smoke", Warhol's appearance was another icon of the age – he is probably the only artist that most people can recognize – and, naturally, he produced a series of prints of himself.

Modern mortality

In his "death-image" series, Warhol examined another facet of contemporary life. He used news photos of accidents, suicides, murders, riots, blowing them up to life size and bigger. Comic strips were another mass-media source to which Warhol turned. But it was Roy Lichtenstein who really exploited their potential. He reproduced the speech bubbles and the narrative panels, the linework and the print quality dot for dot in oil on canvas, twenty times the size of the original.

Tom Wesselmann, like Warhol, was obsessed with supermarket goods, but he set his Coke bottles in banal settings, usually the kitchen. When he moved into the bathrooms though, he often added that traditional artistic icon, the female nude.

Jasper Johns sculpted flashlights, lightbulbs, tins full of paint brushes and beer cans, while Claes Oldenburg built

THE SUNDAY TIMES
COLOUR magazine
JANUARY 26, 1964

THAT'S THE WAY--IT SHOULD HAVE BEGUN! BUT IT'S HOPELESS!

POP ART: way out or way in?

1

the world's biggest hamburgers. George Brecht and Yoko Ono short-circuited the whole process by simply exhibiting household objects themselves. George Segal and Edward Kienholz went one step further, constructing entire domestic, bar or café interiors. Meat cases, pastry stands, entire supermarkets appeared in art galleries. Robert Rauschenburg, who learnt silk-screening from Warhol, summed it up for many of his contemporaries by saying: "I feel that a painting is more real if it is made out of bits of the real world."

The second wave

A second generation of English Pop artists sprang up in the early sixties. Instead of using collage and cut-up techniques like the Independent Group, they painted pop images straight, usually in bold, sometimes clashing colours, rather than juxtaposing them to make an intellectual point. Unlike the earlier generation, they took machines, advertising and mass communications for granted and did not feel the need to analyze them as the IG had done.

David Hockney, Derek Boshier, Patrick Caulfield, Peter Phillips, Allen Jones and Ron Kitaj all emerged at the 1961 Young Contemporaries exhibition. Most of these artists had been at London's Royal College of Art, but they really hit the headlines with their New Generation exhibition at the Whitechapel Gallery in 1964. Hockney himself experimented with Typhoo Tea and Alka-Seltzer packs before going on to develop his own unique deadpan style.

Again the aim was to take art out of the guilt-ridden grip of the old intellectual elite and on to the streets of the modern world. Consumer goods were beautiful – after all they had been created by teams of designers and market researchers whose aim was to make them appeal to a mass market. It was no longer any good producing art that spoke only to a small educated coterie. Pop Art – like pop music – was designed to reach the broad mass of people who had no training in art at all.

1 Roy Lichtenstein blew up the cheap printing techniques of pulp sci-fi comics to Michelangelesque scale. These images popped up everywhere, including the front cover of the Sunday Times *new colour supplement.*

2 David Hockney, one of the second generation of Pop artists in Britain, soon migrated to Los Angeles, his spiritual home. He painted California Bank *in 1964.*

2

Op Art

Bridget Riley, Peter Sedgley, Richard Anuszkiewicz and Piero Dorazio took another path. They developed the eye-aching ideas of Victor Vasarély to arrive at Op Art. Simple visual tricks also had a direct appeal and the swirling geometric patterns in black and white of Bridget Riley, for example, soon made their appearance in fashions and fabrics of the sixties as well as on the walls of art galleries.

Another way these artists tried to take art to the people was the "Happening". The term was originally coined by performance artist Allan Kaprow, who put on '18 Happenings in 6 Parts' in the autumn of 1959. It soon became the media word for any wacky event from artists digging holes and wrapping mountains in cellophane to nude cello recitals and the public smashing of pianos. Established pop artists like Claes Oldenburg and Jim Dine began staging Happenings. These events took a wide variety of forms. Sometimes they were extemporized monologues, sometimes they were improvised plays and scripted theatrical events. What they had in common was a lack of traditional dramatic structure and the fact that they showed to a small audience on a limited run of as little as one or two performances.

In the spirit of the time they tended to include a lot of nudity, which attracted a great deal of media attention. In many ways these Happenings sprung more from the random impulse than the Abstract-Expressionist tradition. What made it Pop was the media attention. And because so few people got to see a Happening themselves, the wild rumours that spread about them were Pop phenomena themselves. High culture and Pop culture were becoming the same thing.

Two cultures become one

Warhol summed up this cross-fertilization better than anyone when he said: "The old idea used to be that intellectuals didn't know what was going on in the other society – popular culture. Those scenes in early rock-and-roll movies were so dated now, where old fogies would hear rock and roll for the first time and start tapping their feet and say, 'That's catchy. What did you say you called it? 'Rock and...roll?'" When Thomas Hoving, the director of the Metropolitan, talked about an exhibit there that included three busts of ancient Egyptian princesses, he referred to them offhandedly as "The Supremes". Everybody was part of the same culture now.

3 Bridget Riley, the doyenne of Op Art. Her scintillating images appeared on curtains, dresses, wallpapers, posters and record sleeves as well as on the walls of art galleries. Op Art was a short-lived phenomenon, though.

3

4

4 Like Andy Warhol, David Hockney had very self-consciously created image. A product of the no-nonsense north of England, he did not hide his homosexuality and became a media star.

INSPIRATIONS

1 *Youth was in, so was space. So artists took their inspiration from science fiction comics.*

2 *The marketing and advertising of products became slick and professional. Commercial artists honed images that they knew meant something to the consumer. Fine artists simply borrowed what worked – to the outrage of the establishment.*

3 *Coca-Cola was not just a drink, it was an important part of American foreign policy. If you could persuade people to drink Coke they were less likely to "go Commie". Pop artists simply picked up on what was already there.*

4 *The work of Italian futurist Gino Severini was halfway between pointillism and Op Art. The futurists also celebrated machinery and the modern world, just as Pop was to do.*

5 *Obsession with the female nude reached new heights in the sixties – on the bookstalls at least. Most punters preferred much more realistic presentation of the nude than this one,* Nude Descending a Staircase, *by Marcel Duchamp. Artists like Allen Jones picked up on this almost fetishistic use of the female nude.*

6 *Pop Art was born neither in the sixties, nor in the habitat one might have expected, America. This collage –* Just What is it That Makes Today's Home so Different, so Appealing *– was created by British artist Richard Hamilton in 1956.*

7 *Henry Moore was still an influential figure among sixties' sculptors. This* Recumbent Figure *was made in 1938. In 1968 the figure was thrown away and only the hole was kept.*

6

5

7

EUROPEAN POP ART

1

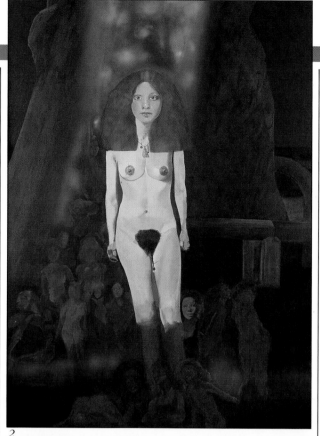

2

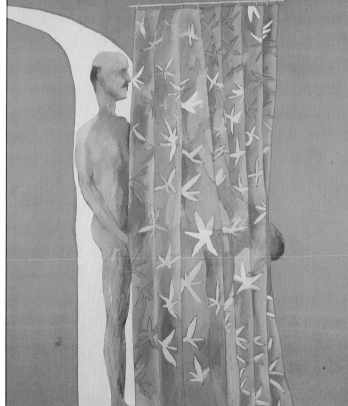

3

1 *While David Hockney was open about his homosexuality, Allen Jones explored his heterosexual obsessions as in this work* First Steps. *He liked long legs in sheer stockings. Later, his airbrushed women would be clad in shiny rubber suits.*

2 *Peter Blake's* Titania. *Blake was a very independent spirit. He was, though, never a member of the Independent Group, nor did he attend any of their exhibitions. Importantly, he was one of the first to turn his back on abstract expressionism. Some of his early work heralded the kind of staged realism that David Hockney went* on *to make famous. Blake turned instead to Pop collage when he designed the influential cover for the Beatles'* Sergeant Pepper's Lonely Hearts Club Band *album in 1967.*

3 *David Hockney was one of a number of pop artists who seemed obsessed with the shower, as in this painting* Two Men in a Shower. *To the British, the shower was still very new, very American. Tom Wesselmann, an American, preferred to put female nudes in his. It was the stuff of advertising.*

4 Calcium Light Night *by Eduardo Paolozzi. Paolozzi was one of the leading members of the Independent Group. His sculpture was inspired by Jean Dubuffet and his collages were influenced by Surrealism, though he anticipated Pop by incorporating many contemporary images.*

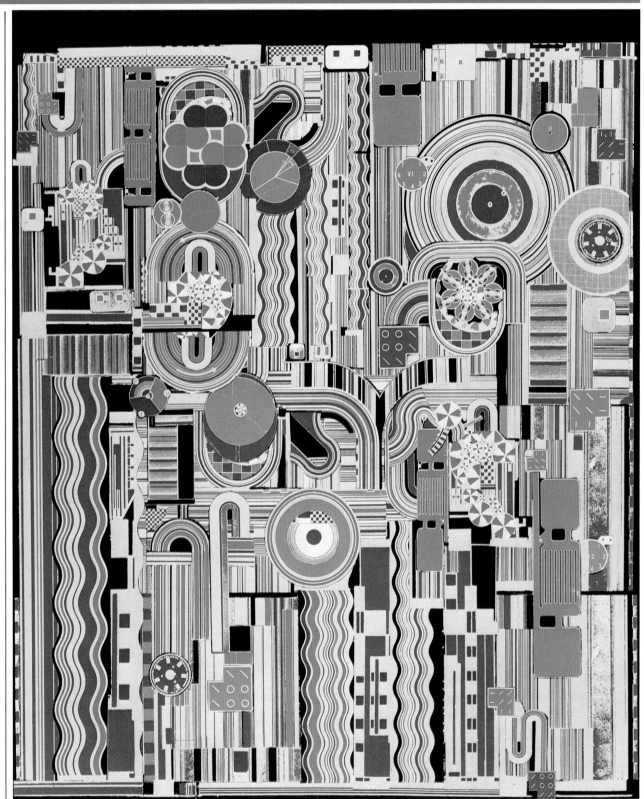

4

U.S. POP ART

1 *Tom Wesselmann's* Still Life *– a spray-painted vacuum-formed tableau with interior illumination. The kitchen and the bathroom came to the art gallery.*

2 *Roy Lichtenstein's* Whaam!, *hand painted in 1963, took the Pop fad for comic books all the way. He painted them big and dot for dot.*

3 *Andy Warhol was not the first Pop artist to use Marilyn Monroe as an icon. John McHale had done it in 1956. Warhol's* Marilyn Diptych *was made in 1962.*

1

2

3

SCULPTURE

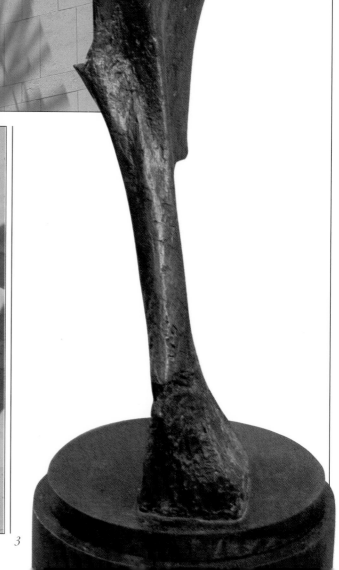

1 Un Sculpture *by Ezio Martinelli, 1962. The use of metal, scrap and other materials shunned by traditional sculpture became trendy in the sixties.*

2 *In Britain, Barbara Hepworth experimented with new materials, but kept some traditional reference points. Her* Winged Figure *adorns the exterior of the John Lewis department store in London's Oxford Street.*

3 *Art school teachers told their students that Pop Art was just a passing fad and mainstream sculptors continued to produce traditional sculptures like this undistinguished bronze abstract figure. The neo-brutalists' aim was to remain 'true to the material'.*

4 *Claes Oldenburg and others reverted to the nihilism of Dada. This* Soft Blue Drainpipe *was made in 1967 and now belongs to the Tate Gallery, London.*

5 Two Figures (Menhirs) *by Barbara Hepworth, 1964. Although using a traditional material, slate, Hepworth chose, in keeping with the ostentatious spirit of the times, to transform her small organic pieces of the forties and fifties into giant structures.*

4

5

53

OP ART

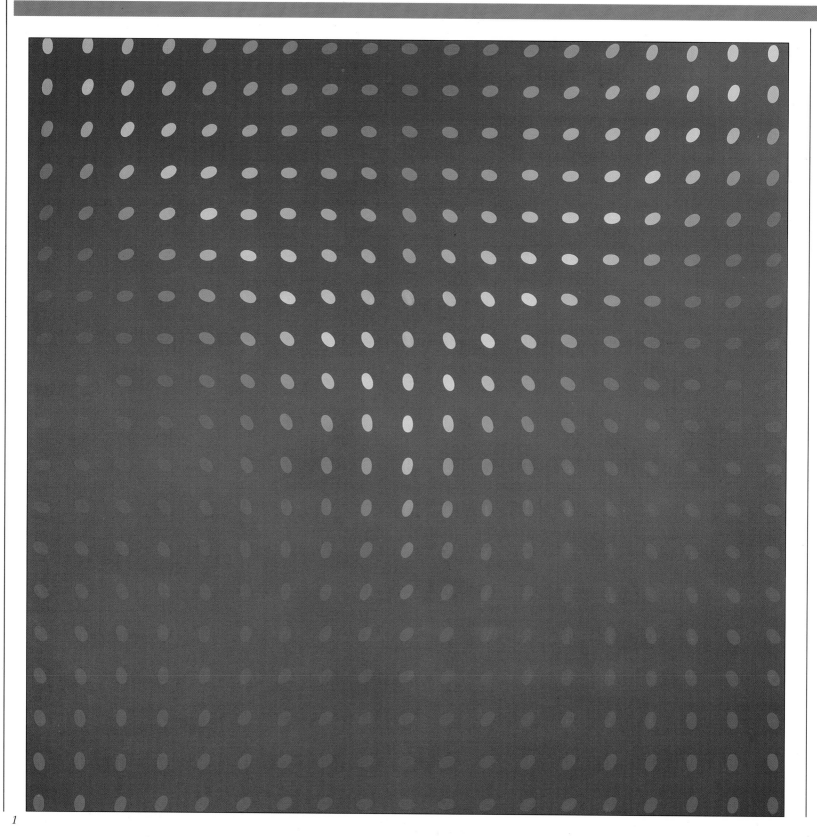

2

3

4

1 *Bridget Riley, the doyenne of Op Art, took Vasarely's geometric ideas and went monochrome. Even a relatively subtle work such as* Deny II *made the eyes go funny.*

2 *Bridget Riley's* Blaze, *from 1962, upset the sensitive retina. But sixties people wanted stimulation whatever the cost. The Jazz of these zig-zag lines appealed to the amphetamine eyes of the early sixties, the way psychedelic patterns appealed to the acid freaks later in the decade.*

3 *Victor Vasarely's straight, simplistic style led the way.* Banya, *shown here, is typical. These primary colours and geometric patterns soon moved from the walls of art galleries to the walls of ordinary homes – as wallpaper and curtain fabric.*

4 *Frank Stella's* Hyena Stomp, *1962, attempted to keep colours fresh, while creating an illusion of space. The title even suggests a certain ethnic influence, which was also becoming chic in the sixties.*

Twiggy posing in a midi coat.

CHAPTER·THREE
GROOVY GEAR

"...the torch has been passed to a new generation..."

JOHN F. KENNEDY

INTRODUCTION

The mini-skirt did it all. It overthrew the autocratic rule of the Paris fashion houses. It shocked and upset the older generation. It gave women a new sense of freedom and it was sexy beyond men's wildest dreams.

The term "mini-skirt" was not widely used until 1965, but hemlines had been rising steadily since the beginning of the decade. It was the brain-child of designer Mary Quant, who had opened her first "Bazaar" boutique in London's Kings Road in 1955. She was one of the success stories of the sixties. In 1961, she opened her second store, in Knightsbridge, and went into wholesale. In 1962, she visited the US and began designing for the J.C. Penney chain. In 1966, she moved into cosmetics and by the end of the decade Quant's daisy logo was seen on everything from bedlinen to stationery. Even her short, angular, Vidal Sassoon haircut was widely copied.

An ear to the ground

What made Quant successful was her unique understanding of the burgeoning youth market. Between 1945 and 1960 the wages of British teenagers had risen twice as fast as those of adults. Without mortgages and families to support, teenagers were eager to spend money on music, on going out and above all on clothes. And they did not want to wear things from the chain stores that catered to their parents' generation.

In the casual atmosphere of small boutiques, designers like Quant could listen to young people and learn what this new clientele wanted. In the sixties, designers did not lead the fashion, they followed it. Top sixties model Twiggy recalls that people often used to make their own clothes because styles were never "in" long enough for the fashion establishment to catch up. The same thing was happening in America. There designers – like Rudi Gernreich – found themselves following rather than leading. "What I do is watch what the kids are putting together for themselves," he said. "I formalize it, give it something of my own, perhaps, and then it is fashion."

Conventional clothes manufacturers complained that the garments produced by Mary Quant and the other new designers were not well made. But this was hardly relevant: clothes were no longer meant to last, because fashion changed too quickly. Paper clothes had a brief vogue, but they were sold in the novelty rather than the fashion departments of big stores.

Other unconventional materials were used too. PVC was hailed as the pop material, because it was new and had

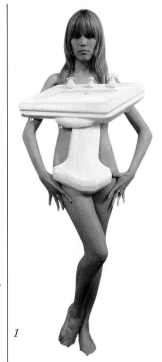

1

1 Not all outfits of the time were this eccentric – or this revealing. But the 1930s ideas of the Surrealist artist Salvador Dali were revived in fashions of the sixties.

2 The boutique owners of London and New York overturned the tyranny of the old-established Paris fashion houses in the early part of the sixties. As the decade progressed, Paris struck back – once again seizing the initiative in style. These coats were designed by Marc Bohan for Dior. The problem was that the new generation could not afford the originals and local sweatshops could get passable copies into the high-street stores before the fashion houses could.

2

3 *The major advance socially and in fashion was the breaking down of traditional sex roles. Men wore their hair long; women adopted the trouser suit. There were problems at first, but soon even the most conservative of environments accepted them.*

4 *Suits were never out – they just took on a new look. The collars could be cropped, like Beatle jackets, the lapels could be widened or there could be more buttons than were really warranted – anything to make the age-old suit seem young, vital and fresh. This one is modelled by stylish sixties photographer Patrick Lichfield.*

5 *PVC was one of the new materials designers latched on to in the sixties. It was a new medium for them to use, unencumbered with the legacy of the past. The old-fashioned kipper tie was beginning to make its re-appearance, too.*

6 *Anything and everything went in the sixties. It did not matter where the colours or patterns came from, just as long as they were bright.*

3

to be used in new ways. Metal was used too, as the space race began to seize the popular imagination.

The traditional division of clothes into formal and casual began to weaken. Young people were supposed to be always on the go and the aim was to come up with clothes that would look good in any situation. One of the innovations that women found particularly adaptable was the trouser suit.

A weekly style briefing

TV pop programmes like *Ready, Steady, Go* lead the pace. Every week kids all over Britain could see the latest trends in music, dance, slang, attitude and dress. Once the hemline had passed the knee, young girls across the country hitched their skirts higher and higher. By the time Twiggy stepped off the plane in a stunned America, mini-skirts had reached mid thigh. By the end of the decade – despite the attempts of couturiers to bring in the maxi-skirt – they had become a crotch-level pelmet, then found they could only go shorter by transmogrifying into "hot pants".

But it was not only thighs that were exposed. In 1964, Rudi Gernreich came up with the topless swim suit. Topless and see-through clothes followed, though only the see-through blouse ever caught on.

6

Although these clothes were designed to be sexy, on ultra-thin models like Twiggy they had a curious innocence. Some of Mary Quant's dresses consciously aped schoolgirls' gym slips. The mature figure of the fifties was definitely out. To have the sylph-like form of an adolescent was everything for fashion conscious women. Andy Warhol pointed out that, with all the slimming pills and amphetamines people took to stay awake, most people ended the sixties younger than when they had started the decade. In Britain, Barbara Hulanicki – the designer behind Biba – believed that the girls who wore Biba clothes "were post-war babies who had been deprived of nourishing protein in childhood and grew up into beautiful skinny people. A designer's dream."

The Mod look
For men, too, the muscular torso of the American footballer was out. The slim, almost androgynous, look of the adolescent was in. This style began in England with the Mods. They spent the money from their daytime jobs on tight-fitting Italian suits, American army-surplus parkas and the all-important scooter. At night and weekends they

took "purple hearts" to help them party. These, again, kept them thin. The slim, smooth Mod look was later exported to America by the Beatles and the other British bands. It has been said that Mick Jagger single-handedly changed the American idea of masculine beauty.

By the mid-sixties Paris began to strike back. The old established houses like Dior and Balenciaga had given up the struggle and catered exclusively to their older clientele, but young turks like André Courrèges and Paco Rabanne started designing trendy clothes in metal and plastic. And Pierre Cardin pioneered the unisex look. The problem was that they had trouble holding on to their ideas. Even though these younger houses went into ready-to-wear fashions, there were others who could get cheap imitations into the shops faster. Copies of Yves Saint Laurent's 1965 Mondrian collection were on sale all over England within weeks.

While the girls looked to Chelsea's Kings Road for their fashions, men flocked to Carnaby Street. Just the other side of Regent Street from the traditional heart of British men's tailoring, Savile Row – Savile Row is posh Mayfair while Carnaby Street is in Bohemian Soho – Carnaby Street became the centre of modern men's style largely due to the efforts of John Stephen. A Glaswegian, he opened his first shop there in 1957 when he was 19, selling Italian suits. By the mid-sixties he had expanded, owning a string of shops down Carnaby Street retailing his own range of clothes.

Determined to overthrow the "staid, sober and, above all, correct" form of dress that advertised "your precise rung on the social ladder and even your bank account", Stephen produced clothes which – in 1962 at least – were even considered effeminate. To counter this he took the step of employing the up-and-coming British boxer Billy Walker as a model. No one dared cast aspersions on his manhood, even when he was swathed from head to foot in pink denim.

Hair – the parting of the waves
In shoes, the ultra-pointed winklepickers gave way to chisel toes and elastic-sided Chelsea boots. The greasy, slicked-back hair of the Teddy boys and bikers gave way to the shorter, sharper hairstyles of the Mods.

Once the Beatles had popularized the Mod look on both sides of the Atlantic with their sharp suits and pudding basin haircuts, the Rolling Stones took the casual couldn't-care-less look of the Beatniks and reworked it with more style and colour. Their dress was flamboyant, rebellious, unisex. Lead singer Mick Jagger even donned an organdie mini-dress for the band's free concert in London's Hyde Park in 1969.

The Rolling Stones' hair was long, and grew longer. So did the Beatles'. Girls, who had given up the "beehives" and bubbly styles of the fifties for the shiny, straight bobs

1 Pierre Cardin was of the generation of younger designers who decided to fight back with ready-to-wear fashion. These space-age creations come from his 1967 collection.

2 Dutch designers The Fool dressed the Beatles in 1967. Their aim was not to make money but to turn people on.

3 The tight ski-pants of the fifties gradually gave way to flares, bell-bottoms, then loon pants. Bright colours, novel materials, chunky rings and sports cars were all part of the sixties look. Fashion photographers also liked castles and old-world settings to heighten the effect of the latest fashions.

1

4 *The day the "Shrimp" shocked Australia. On 5 November, 1965, 22-year-old model Jean Shrimpton turned up at the Melbourne races with no hat, no gloves, no stockings and a shift that stopped four inches (10cm) above her knees!*

ERNESTINE CARTER ON THE PARIS COLLECTIONS: COURREGES V. THE REST

5 *The glossy women's magazines saw it as Courrèges against the rest. André Courrèges was the first of the Paris couturiers to take up the challenge of the sixties. In 1964 he produced a space-age collection which established white and silver as the season's colours. Here his relaxed young fashions, on the left, are contrasted with the more formal styles of Dior, centre, and Ricci, right.*

of Vidal Sassoon, let their hair grow out too. By 1967, lanky, tousled hair became the very symbol of youthful rebellion and, in the USA, of opposition to the war being fought in Vietnam, which was, after all, being waged by crew-cut generals and shaven-headed rookies. Meanwhile, Blacks were giving up the gunk and grease that had helped mould their hair into mock-white styles and instead teased out huge "Afros", a symbol of black pride in their African heritage. Eventually, even the US Marine Corps allowed black troops to wear a modified version of the Afro.

Beads, bell-bottoms and beatitude

The anti-war movement spawned the hippies, who looked to the East for their non-violent philosophy – and for their clothes. For women there were long, flowing skirts in intricate cotton prints. For both sexes, Indian kaftans, headbands, "love beads", bells and bell-bottomed hipsters were the thing. Hipsters were unisex trousers that rested on the hips rather than on the waist, though a wide belt with a heavy buckle was often added as adornment.

In 1969, when the Beatles and other luminaries went to India to meditate with the Maharishi Mahesh Yogi, they gave this would-be spiritual movement the official seal. Guru-esque beards sprouted on every male chin. Women either took the ascetic route and wore no make-up at all – or they went over the top with wild, theatrical make-up, often with the peace symbol, a flower, painted on their faces. It was also not unknown, most likely under the influence of drugs, for men to paint flowers on their faces, too.

During this psychedelic phase, many of the Beatles'

clothes were designed by a group of young Dutch artists – Simon Posthuma, Josje Leeger, Marijke Koger and Barrie Finch – known collectively as The Fool. They mixed and matched colours and styles from every culture. "Our ideas come from India, China, Russia, Turkey and from the sixteenth to the twenty-first centuries. There's a bit of everything," they said. In practice, many hippies put together their own unique "total look" from items they found in second-hand markets.

It was inevitable that hippy fashions should find their way into the straight world too. Suits with flared hipster trousers and flamboyantly waisted jackets came in, along with psychedelic and flowered shirts and kipper ties, often in the same fabric as the shirt.

Tee-shirts – the great leveller

Jeans – flared, parallel or excruciatingly tight – and tee-shirts – plain white, bell-sleeved, perhaps brandishing the name of a band or the image of Che Guevara on the front – came through it all as the democratic dress of the decade. The tee-shirt and jeans even triumphed where a tie was once compulsory.

Many of these trends were taken to even greater extremes in the seventies and have even been seen in the eighties. In the early sixties, youngsters found that they could pick up old-fashioned army-surplus clothing cheaply in West London's Portobello Road street market. The Beatles wore stylized army uniforms on the cover of their 1967 album *Sergeant Pepper's Lonely Hearts Club Band* and on tour. In the late eighties, Michael Jackson adopted a similar look after making his album and video *Thriller*.

INSPIRATIONS

1

2

3

4

1 Marlon Brando in jeans and a leather jacket in The Wild One *(1953) was a fashion image that would not go away. The motorcycle gangs transformed themselves into Hell's Angels while the Mods went to the opposite extreme in Italian suits, only to revert to jeans as the sixties wore on.*

2 Disaffection with the consumer society in the late sixties opened fashion to all sorts of Third World influences.

3 Biba brought back the twenties flapper dress – their hemlines, too, had scandalized the twenties just as the mini-skirts of the sixties scandalized their own decade.

4 Stores selling army surplus were raided for greatcoats, berets, camouflage fatigues and other gear.

5 *Mondrian's positive use of primary colours was much emulated in sixties' fashion. His designs, too, turned up on dresses and curtain material.*

6 *Pop stars travelling to India to practise transcendental meditation and students on the hippy trail brought back with them the influences of the East.*

7 *Oxford Bags did not come back, but they might as well have done. The flared trousers that came in at the end of the sixties stretched to similarly loony proportions below the knee.*

MINI, MIDI, MAXI

1 *1968, and the hemlines were creeping higher. Coloured tights were a must, but the overall look is still innocent and school-girlish.*

2 *Even for evening wear, the mini-skirt was the thing. The hemlines had retreated dramatically since 1965, but no one was shocked now.*

3 *Twiggy had the perfect pre-pubescent figure. No matter how revealing the skirt, she still looked innocent. Her ultra-thin, schoolgirl looks made her instantly recognizable the world over.*

4 *Towards the end of the decade, hemlines plunged down again. But the mini was not replaced by the midi or the maxi. These coats – inspired by the movie Dr Zhivago – kept legs exposed by mini-skirts warm in winter.*

1

2

3

4

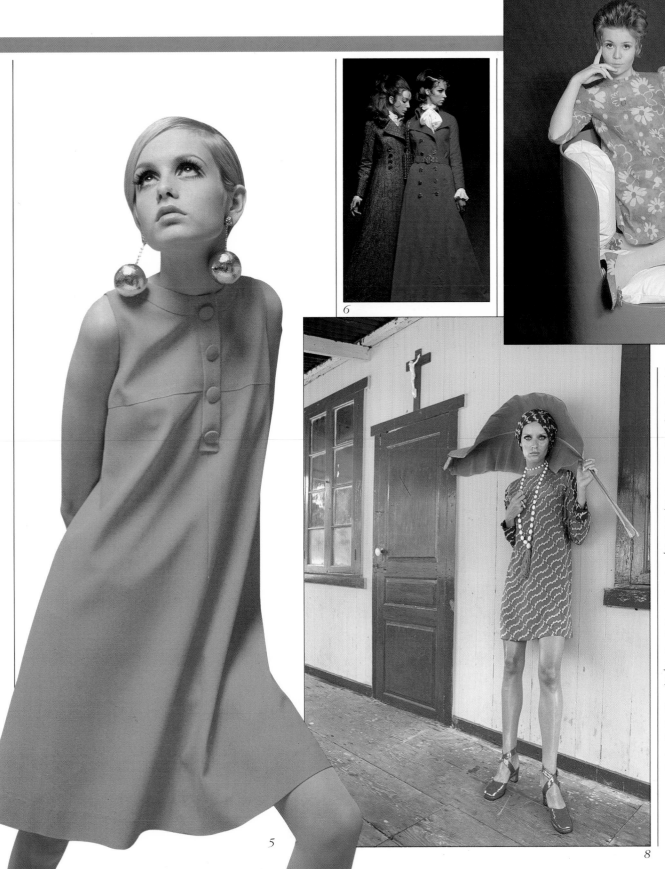

5

6

7

8

5 *Even sophisticated evening outfits and heavy make-up could not persuade us that Twiggy was grown up. The huge silver earrings – very fashionable in 1966 – make her look even more of an innocent in a knowing world.*

6 *Classic styles – albeit theatrically presented – made a comeback, courtesy of Biba, the top sixties boutique. These maxi coats are from 1968.*

7 *In 1967, Flower Power was already on its way. The motif was used on this Mod mini dress and the matching shoes before Flower Children proper, with their free love and pot, took over. The paper flowers were very Mod, as was the plastic chair.*

8 *The Afro-Asian styles that had inspired the hippies spilled over into the Mod movement. But for 1969, this outfit is positively conservative.*

NEW MATERIALS

1 The inspiration is space travel and Op Art. Pierre Cardin picked black and silver as the colours for his 1969 collection. The man's outfit is leather. The woman's dress is of printed silk.

2 PVC was practical, especially in "Swinging London". It took Op Art patterns well and, in 1966 designers realized that it cut and hung like no material ever used before.

3 Italian-born Emmanuel Ungaro followed in the footsteps of Courrèges with his crisp, tailored look. In 1969, he pushed things to the limit, creating a collection that was a cross between clothes and body jewellery.

4 *The midi length – even in modern materials – never really took off. The supremacy of the mini only waned with the long, loose look of the Flower Children – and even then hot pants were still to come.*

5 *Spanish architect turned fashion designer Paco Rabanne used metal and plastic cut into strips or discs and wired together. His first Paris collection of these futuristic garments was in 1966. This metallic dress suits the black skin of model Donyale Luna particularly well. The dramatic pose was devised by Salvador Dali.*

4

5

SWINGING LONDON

THE HEAD SHOP 202 KENSINGTON PARK RD, W.11.

2 The hippies moved the action out of the centre of town, back to the more relaxed parts of west London, such as the traditionally bohemian area around Portobello Road, W11.

3 England was swinging and the Union Jack itself became a Pop icon that appeared on dresses, tee-shirts, jackets, mugs and posters.

1 Carnaby Street was where it was happening, especially for men's clothes. Lord John was the first boutique in the narrow Soho street, just a stone's throw from the traditional heart of men's tailoring, Savile Row.

1

3

4

4 *At the centre of the fashion revolution that was taking place in London were the boutiques. Biba opened its doors in 1964. Run by Barbara Hulanicki and her husband Stephen Fitzsimon, its dark interior throbbed with pop music and fast, expendable fashion ideas. Children were catered for, too. In 1969, Biba abandoned its Art Nouveau logo for an Art Deco one when it transformed itself from a small boutique into a vast department store.*

5 *I Was Lord Kitchener's Valet, in Portobello Road's antique market, sold old army uniforms. These went in and out of fashion throughout the sixties. Mick Jagger and the Beatles were all seen in army gear at some time.*

5

THEATRICAL FASHION

1 Bernard La Vin in a sleeveless blue velvet dinner jacket suit that has a quaintly Victorian look. Frances Crahay's evening dress by Jules has a distinctly West African look.

2 Rupert Lycett Green – with his wife Claudia – in a raw-silk evening suit from Blades.

3 Op Art patterns made dramatic effects.

4 Michael Fish of Mr Fish in a purple silk tunic jacket and poplin roll-neck.

5 *Mick Jagger was fond of outfits inspired by army uniforms of the past. By 1967, it was difficult to pick up original examples. Jagger was always one of the leaders of fashion. His slim, androgynous look put the body builders and men built like American football players in the shade for more than a decade. The uniform motif also appeared that year on the cover of the Beatles' album* Sergeant Pepper's Lonely Hearts Club Band.

6 *Hylan Booker went as far back as Maid Marion for inspiration for this brown organza dress he designed for Worth. These fantasy creations were fun and filled the pages of the fashion magazines, but they had little currency on the streets. They were expensive and could be worn only once or twice to fashionable parties or exclusive venues. It was all part of the process that took fashion out of the hands of the kids and put it back in the control of the couturiers again.*

5

6

SEE-THROUGH AND TOPLESS

1

2

3

1 *Thin, lacy tops worn with or without a bra accounted for a lot of careless driving during the sixties.*

2 *However revealing the blouse, the important thing was to retain that quintessential innocence.*

3 *The first topless dress to hit Australia, though it is worn here with a lacy bra. The outfit also features a split skirt showing off the leg, but the overall effect is quite conservative. It would have to be. The price of the ensemble was 50 guineas (£52.50) – expensive for those days.*

4 *Even the British high-street group of stores, Wallace Heaton, caught on to the see-through look. Chains and decorations were often used to obscure the important bits and women often wore a flesh-coloured body stocking to spare their blushes.*

5 *Then there was the topless look. These dresses hit the news when models and actresses wore them, but they never caught on in a big way. This dress was on sale for $36, and sold well.*

4

5

HIPPY LOOK

1 *The flower motif of the hippies was rapidly taken up by mainstream fashion. This brocade mini-coat, made in London in 1967, cashed in on the Flower Power movement that was spreading eastwards across the world from San Francisco's Haight Ashbury district.*

2 *August 1967 – it was early yet for hippies in London and the fashions still retain elements of the Mod look. But the major themes are there – long, tangled hair, psychedelic and paisley patterns, badges, the return of jeans, organic food and references to the drug culture.*

3 *The trousers are hipsters, sitting on the hips rather than on the waist. The scarves are flowing and romantic, the hair long and the belts wide. She is still wearing a mini, but the flower says it all. This is 1967 and the Summer of Love.*

4 And the Beatles went hippy too. Surprisingly, it was not John Lennon who led the way. Pictured here in 1967, he is still in high Mod gear – suit and white shirt with matching tie. But the other three are dressed in Indian cotton shirts. George's brocade jacket has a distinctly Eastern feel, but Ringo has gone all the way. He is wearing a sleeveless Afghan jacket and "love beads"!

5 With Flower Power going on in the background, "overground" fashion became more way out too. Traces of Mod are still there, but the look is altogether looser and more laid-back.

6 Mad make-up did not begin in 1967, but face and body painting took off with the hippies. Painted clown faces, psychedelic swirls and the ubiquitous flower began to appear on faces at pop festivals and love-ins.

4

5

6

JEWELRY

1 Heavy rings with fantastic and oriental designs were the fashion in the sixties – even in the mainstream gold and diamond market. These wedding rings, with their heavily textured and encrusted finishes, were made by Charles de Temple, the London-based son of Tom Mix, the legendary Hollywood cowboy.

3 This simple, stark gold pendant, designed by Bent Gabrielson Pederson, is typical of the Scandinavian style. Although Scandinavian jewellers had been coming up with designs like this for some time, the primitive, ethnic feel struck a particular chord in the sixties. Black models were often used to display this jewellery.

2 An important figure in the development of the innovative and extravagant ideas that were so much in vogue at the time was John Donald. The natural crystalline form of the rutilated quartz is echoed in the gold surround.

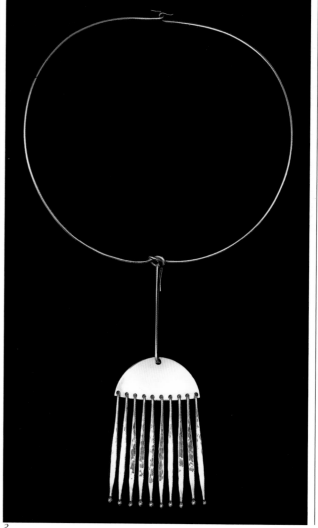

5 *The sixties saw the rapid spread of the cult of leisure, and jewellery buyers were supposed to boast a knowledge of the arts when making their choice. This brooch, by Gillian Packard, plainly owes something to Mondrian, or to the bas-relief pictures of Ben Nicholson, with its squares of different-coloured gold, emeralds and diamonds.*

5

4

6

4 *So why should jewellery be confined to fingers, necks and ear lobes? French sculptor Gustin welded together these feathered trousers. The necklace-breastplace-belt was designed by Emmanuel Ungaro in 1969. With jewellery like this, who needs clothes?*

6 *Even this high-street jewellery, sold by the British clothing chain Wallace Heaton, shows distinctly Eastern influences. Indians were settling in Britain in numbers for the first time and bringing with them their unique culture. The Beatles, other sixties luminaries and those seeking enlightenment on the hippy trail, all helped make the oriental fashionable.*

HAIR

1 Hair was all important in the sixties. Even when it was overshadowed by make-up, psychedelic-patterned clothes and coloured contact lenses, it was still an individual's crowning glory.

4 Vidal Sassoon was the most influential hairdresser of the era. His short, practical cuts, with their chic, angular shapes, were much copied. Modern girls easily abandoned the longer, spray-saturated styles of the fifites in favour of shorter cuts that would look good at work and needed no attention if they wanted to go on to a party after.

1

2

2 Despite the egalitarian spirit of the age, "debs" still had their own styles, which owed more to their mothers than to Vidal Sassoon.

3

3 Doris Day had many followers, the parents of the sixties young in particular appreciating her virginal look.

4

5

6 *As the hippy look came in, long, natural-looking hair, glossy with protein conditioner, took over from the Soigné look of the Mods. It went better with nudity and the surreal timelessness of the new jewellery.*

9 *Long, loose and luxuriant. Hair was the thing on the stage and in the street. Natural, unkempt and hippy was great – but a few braids to make it ethnic was even better. This was the era of civil rights. And if you had to have a hat, why not look like Wyatt Earp dressed by the local thrift shop?*

6

7

5 *Strong colours were the name of the game – in hair as well as clothes. And if that meant you had to wear a wig, so much the better. There was no shame in that. In the sixties, everything had to be obvious and out in the open.*

7 *Hair was always more than an accessory. When it was blond and pulled up, it did not matter that your mascara and your eyebrows were black, just as long as your dog collar had something less than a religious look.*

8 *If you could not get hold of the real thing, you could always wear plastic flowers in your hair.*

8

9

Monorail from the Seattle World Fair.

CHAPTER · FOUR
HARDWARE

*"That's one small step for man, one giant
leap for mankind."*

NEIL ARMSTRONG

INTRODUCTION

The sixties' very own triumph of industrial design was the conquest of space, although the first satellite, the Soviet Union's Sputnik, had been launched into orbit in 1957 and much of the technology in the early space programme had come from the German efforts towards the end of the war to develop the V2 rocket.

However, it was not until the Russians fired the first man, Yuri Gagarin, into space in 1961 that the space race really began. President Kennedy's response was a promise to put a man on the moon by the end of the decade. America lived up to his promise. Its effort cost $23 billion and the lives of three astronauts, burnt to death during a launchpad test. The giant Saturn 5 rockets that powered the moon mission, the tiny instrument-crammed Apollo capsules, the leggy lunar lander and the innovative designs of prototype lunar buggies all had an enormous influence on the hardware of our everyday lives.

Spin-offs of the space race

New technology and design concerns from the space programme flooded into other industries. Packing so much vital instrumentation, control and life-support equipment into tiny space capsules where men would have to live for days on end stimulated a new interest in ergonomics, the science of matching machines to human needs. With "human engineering" in mind, designers looked at furniture, cars, aircraft and domestic appliances with a new eye, tailoring them better to human dimensions and the range of human movements.

The original work on ergonomics was done by Henry Dreyfuss who, when working on the interior design of a new American tank, drew up a series of "anthropometric charts" showing the human body in a variety of different positions. Dreyfuss went on to work with X-rays of the human spine to develop seats for the Lockheed JetStar executive jet and his ideas spread into every area of product design and engineering.

To help in the design of new mattresses, bed manufacturers used hundreds of pictures of a man rolling about during sleep. Japanese National Railways applied ergonomics to the design of the driver's cab of their Tokkaido high-speed trains. DAF and Leyland drew on ergonomics for the design of their trucks. Manufacturers of the new high-fidelity – or hi-fi – equipment took a lead from the new science to position the control knobs. Even the lavatory was redesigned anthropometrically.

There were other legacies of the American space programme. The non-stick frying pan is probably the best known. Its Teflon surface was developed to help spacecraft slip more easily through the atmosphere. But the most far-reaching spin-off was the massive advance made in the computing capabilities needed to control and track distant space vehicles. The massive machines of the fifties with their valves and relays were replaced by machines

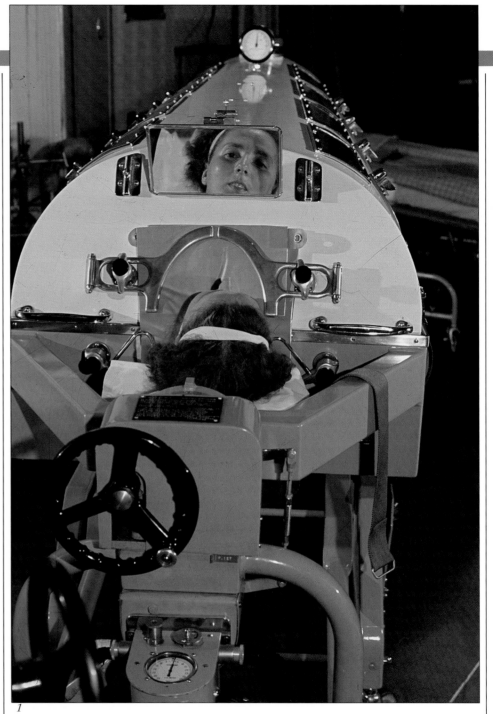

1

1 *Harold Wilson, Britain's prime minister from 1964 to 1974, referred to "the white heat of the technological revolution" that was such a feature of the decade. And there were indeed huge technological advances – especially in medicine and biotechnology, as with the artificial lung (shown here). Transplants – particularly of the heart – made the headlines, but the real progress was made in the field of research. The sixties were also the new age of machinery, a second Industrial Revolution. With men walking on the moon, it seemed that there was no problem that technological muscle could not solve.*

using transistor and magnetic-tape technology, as in the IBM System 360 introduced in 1964, and later by primitive integrated circuits. Olivetti even introduced the world's first desktop computer, the Programma 101, in 1966.

The communications explosion

Another direct beneficiary of the space programme was worldwide communications. The first communication satellite, Telstar, was put up in 1962. The clamour for live coverage of the Olympic Games in 1964 and 1968, and of the Vietnam war, speeded the progress. By 1969, when Neil Armstrong first set foot on the moon, the earth was ringed with satellites and 600 million people could see live pictures of the historic landing and moonwalk on their own TV screen.

In 1960, the Hughes Aircraft Company produced the world's first laser. By 1968, laser light beamed from the Kitt Peak Observatory in Arizona was being detected by the unmanned Surveyor 7 on the moon. Laser light was modulated for communications and the foundations were laid for today's fibre-optic communications systems. Lasers were used to cut metal, repair damaged retinas, treat cancer and to align bridges and dams. And by the end of the decade the first hologram – or laser-lit 3D photograph – was produced.

But however you measured it, the world was becoming a smaller place. The first Boeing 747 rolled off the

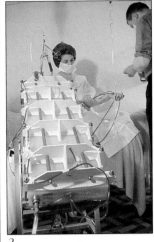

2 *The artificial kidney, or dialysis machine, was one of the great life-saving developments of the decade. It cleansed the blood, just like a real kidney. Unfortunately, patients had to be plugged in every couple of days. But it kept them alive until a suitable kidney donor was found.*

4

3 *Personal mobility was the watchword of the sixties. Raleigh introduced the Wisp, a small-wheel motorcycle with automatic transmission. Top speed was 25mph (40km/hr) and it did 150 miles to the gallon (53km/litre). The cost, a mere 57 guineas (£59.85). Though it had some success in Britain and Europe, it had no chance in the USA.*

4 *High speed was all the rage. Speed limits had not yet been imposed on the motorways. And on the railways, new high-speed technology was being developed. The Japanese were working on their "bullet train" and SNCF were pushing up the speeds on French railways with this 190mph- (300km/hr-) TGV.*

1

1 Bombed into submission just 15 years before the decade started, the Japanese laid the foundation for their economic miracle in that decade. At first, their transistor radios, TVs and motorbikes were derided as cheap imitations of Western designs. But their continuing priority of investment in research and development has seen off competition worldwide in electronics, cars, motorbikes and shipbuilding. Only now are the Japanese feeling the pressure from the developing manufacturing nations of Southeast Asia.

production line in 1969, putting jet travel within reach of many ordinary people for the first time. And for the high-rollers, Concorde made its first flight, shrinking the Atlantic crossing to a mere 3½ hours.

The F-111 jet fighter saw combat for the first time in the air above Vietnam and the American army fighting there was issued with a new lightweight semi-automatic rifle, the M-16. Built largely in plastic and designed to be self-cleaning, it soon became well known to terrorists around the world as the Armalite.

Scaled-down for success

After years of making cars bigger and grander, Detroit ran out of ideas. Britain took things to the other extreme with Alec Issigonis's mini-car and the bubble car. The mini was particularly successful. As far as the British public were concerned it seemed to capture the new youthful, demo-cratic, swinging ethos, as did the Moulton, a new style of folding bicycle with miniature wheels. In 1965, the Toyota Corona eventually broke Detroit's stranglehold on the American market and Japanese cars began selling in the West in ever-increasing numbers.

During the fifties, the Japanese had been notorious for their cheap plastic imitations of western consumer goods. But in the sixties, the design departments of their large corporations began to produce goods that looked good

too. The Japanese were also in the vanguard of the move towards miniaturization. Many of the ubiquitous "trannies" – the name for the miniature transistor radios every teenager carried – came from Japan. And in 1960, Sony produced a battery-operated portable TV with an eight-inch (20cm) screen.

Breaking the loudness barrier

At the sharp end of the entertainment industry, things were moving in the opposite direction. The Beatles went into the sixties using a Grundig tape recorder, set to record with the pause button held down as an amplifier which had a power rating of just four watts. By the time they reached The Cavern, they had the use of a 25-watt amplifier with 12-inch (30cm) speakers. When they played at Shea Stadium, they had 50-watt amplifiers for the bass and PA and 30-watt amplifiers for the guitar – power ratings that these days would not be considered adequate to fill the average church hall.

Then the Who introduced the Marshall stack – a standard valve amplifier sitting on top of two cabinets each containing four 12-inch (30cm) speakers. The race was on to pile up more and more Marshall stacks. By 1967, the Pink Floyd were using an 800-watt PA amplifier. And by the time of Woodstock, in 1969, bands were fronting massive walls of speakers, generating enough audio

2

2 The great sixties achievement of the Japanese was the "tranny". They shrank the traditional Bakelite beast into a pocket-sized plastic fashion item.

84

power to blow away everything for miles.

Although the electric guitar was the symbol of the sixties, it was really perfected in the fifties and saw little development during the following decade. However, in 1964, Dr Robert Moog developed a prototype electronic music synthesizer. Two years later it was on sale to the public and in 1968 the sound of the Moog synthesizer earned worldwide attention with Walter Carlos's album *Switched-on Bach*.

Looks are everything

In consumer products, the look of an item began to assume an overwhelming importance. In some cases even function was sacrificed if the look was right – as in Paul Clark's Pop Art clocks with almost unreadable faces. Electric shavers by Braun and Courier took on a distinctly phallic style.

Stainless steel – in a satin finish as well as the highly polished silver look – was used for kitchenware. Britain's David Mellor designed several ranges of cutlery in stainless steel, most notably the Thrift range which was commissioned by the Ministry of Public Buildings and Works for use in Her Majesty's prisons, in government canteens and by British Rail. Its spoons had shallow bowls, the knives had no division between the blade and the handle and the whole set comprised only five pieces.

The growing mass market for air travel heralded new designs in plastic cutlery and crockery for in-flight meals. David Mellor accordingly came up with a range of plastic cutlery, designed for mass catering and cheap enough to throw away. Oddly enough, disposable plastic even caught on in the home, domestic users often washing it and using it again.

Eastman Kodak began to take a serious look at the styling of their products. In 1961, Hans Gugelot designed the Kodak Carousel slide projector and in 1964 Kenneth Grange was responsible for the look of the Brownie Vecta camera. IBM combined design with new technology and came up with the Selectric typewriter, the first to use the radical "golf-ball" typing head.

Italian styling

But it was Italy that was still way ahead in design technology. Versatile designers like Achille and Pier Giacomo Castiglione, Joe Colombo, Anna Castelli Ferrieri, Marco Zanuso and Ettore Sottsass – many of whom also designed furniture – became international tastemakers in the field of consumer durables. Their approach was stylish but not always serious. The red-plastic pop-styled Valentine typewriter designed by Ettore Sottsass and Perry King for Olivetti was aimed to make office machinery less daunting. Sottsass's bright, chunky office chair, also for Olivetti, was the perfect concomitant, making the workplace young, fun and playful.

3 The great lung-cancer debate was only just beginning during the sixties and the design of cigarette lighters was still very important. The TFG2 Cylindric table lighter, designed in 1969, was produced by Braun. It is pure Modernism.

4 Package holidays and the massive expansion in business travel by air gave caterers new problems. Passengers had to be fed – and the food had to be hot even when the plane was delayed. What was harder still, caterers had to devise a menu that would suit a wide range of tastebuds in a situation where diners did not have the normal distractions of good conversation and a good atmosphere.

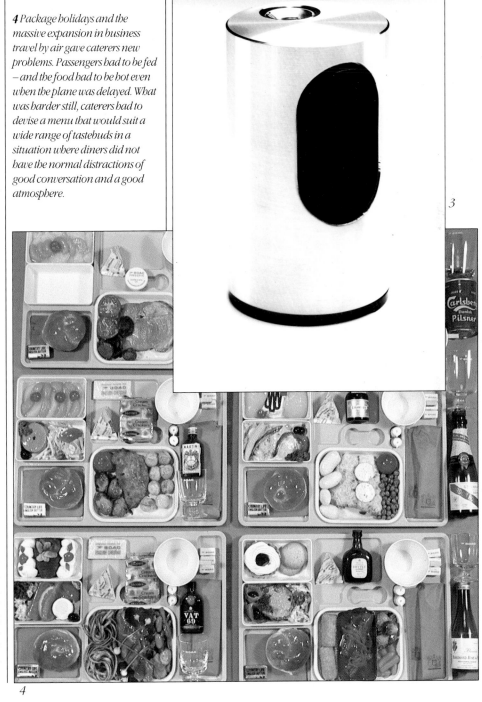

3

4

INSPIRATIONS

1

PARUFAMET   Metropolis.

2

OKV 3

3

1 *The Japanese had taken trees and miniaturized them for centuries. Now they did the same with Western electrical goods, and in the sixties, produced the Bonsai radio – the ubiquitous tranny.*

2 *The Plug-In Cities of Archigram owe much to the 1926 film Metropolis. Hardware manufacturers, too, still liked the heavily industrial look, which they thought of as hi-tech.*

3 *The long sleek lines of the Le Mans winning D-type Jaguar found their way into production cars with the E-type Jaguar and were copied by sports car designers everywhere.*

4 *Braun was something of a leader in the use of interesting design in electrical goods. German and Japanese manufacturers particularly began to employ art-school trained designers, rather than engineers.*

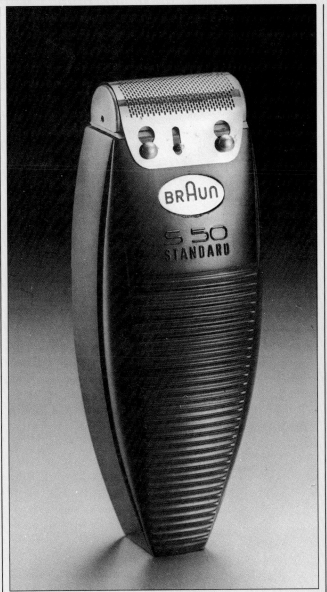

5

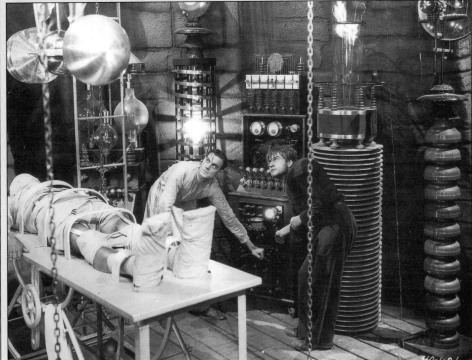

6

4

5,6 *The race for the moon forced the pace of industrial innovation. Spin-offs from the space race quickly found their way into the shops. Manufacturers also incorporated motifs familiar from the space programme but of no technological significance into domestic consumer items.*

7 *In the sixties, everything seemed possible. With heart transplants, kidney machines and medical technology proceeding by leaps and bounds, the cure for cancer – and everything else – seemed just around the corner. The world of Frankenstein – a more up-tempo version than the Mary Shelley novel – was on the very doorstep.*

7

SPACE

1 *Soviet cosmonaut Major Yuri Gagarin, the first man in space, was shot into orbit by a multi-stage rocket from the launch site at Tyura Tam on 12 April, 1961.*

2 *On 18 March, 1965, Soviet cosmonaut Aleksei A. Leonov became the first man to leave an orbiting spacecraft and float in space.*

3 *The lift-off of America's first two-man Gemini spacecraft from Pad 19, Cape Kennedy, Florida, on 23 March, 1965, 9.24 Eastern Standard Time – 24 minutes behind schedule. Under near-perfect skies Gemini 3 carried Virgil "Gus" Grissom and John Young into orbit at a height of 100-140 miles (160-225km).*

1

2

3

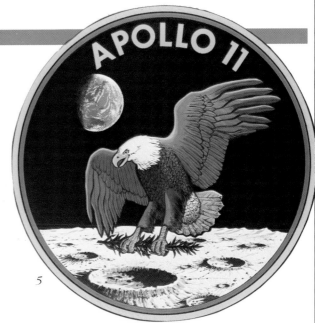

5

4

4 Earth, as seen from the moon – the climax of the most historic achievement of the sixties. This is the view that greeted the crew of Apollo 11 as they came from behind the moon after their "lunar orbit insertion burn", just before their historic landing.

5 The official emblem of the Apollo 11 mission – the first to land on the moon. It is the property of the US government and authorized only for the use of astronauts.

6 Astronaut Edwin E. "Buzz" Aldrin during EVA – extra-vehicular activity – on the moon. The pad of the Lunar Module Eagle, wrapped in gold foil, can be seen, lower right. The boot prints are still there today. The picture was taken by Neil Armstrong with a 70 mm lunar surface camera.

6

1 Exploration of the moon was only one of the objectives of space travel in the sixties. The Mariner series of unmanned space probes were sent to explore other planets in the solar system. This one, Mariner IV, skimmed past Mars on 14 July 1964, giving man his first close-up view of another planet.

2 The vast scale of the engineering required to put man into space is shown in this view of NASA's Manned Spacecraft Center at Cape Canaveral, Florida as the Mercury Atlas 6 rocket blasts off carrying John Glenn in a Friendship 7 spacecraft up for three orbits of the Earth.

1

2

5 *In preparation for the weightlessness of space, astronauts were trained in free-falling aircraft and by floating in swimming pools. American astronauts – like first man on the moon Neil Armstrong shown here – also had to look forward to a landing in the sea on their return to Earth.*

3 *This multiple exposure photograph shows the gantry being lowered as a Titan rocket launches a two-man Gemini spacecraft into orbit on 18 July 1966.*

4 *The development of the space suit was crucial. It had to be absolutely air-tight and sealed to maintain pressure in atmosphereless space. The suit's silvered surface protected the astronaut from harmful radiation. Underneath, underwear veined with a network of fine water pipes provided cooling. This suit is modelled by Alan Shepard – the first American in space. His short up-and-down trip into space on 5 May 1961 lasted only about 15 minutes.*

SPACE SPIN-OFFS

1 *Since Isaac Newton developed his laws of motion in 1687, it had been theoretically possible to send a man to the moon. However, it was not until the development of the computer that the calculations necessary to keep a spacecraft on course on such a trip were possible. In fact, model electronic computers were developed shortly after the Second World War, and the rapid development of their capacity forced by the space programme had huge benefits for the world of commerce.*

2 *The massive main-frame computers of the early sixties, which could only be handled by highly trained programmers, soon gave way to the prototypes of the desktop computers we know today. This is the IBM 1130. Hardly a PC, but all the elements are there.*

3 *The IBM 360 does not look much like the desktop models of today. But in 1964 it was the first office computer to use the modern transistor-and-tape technology. Microchips were just around the corner.*

1

2

3

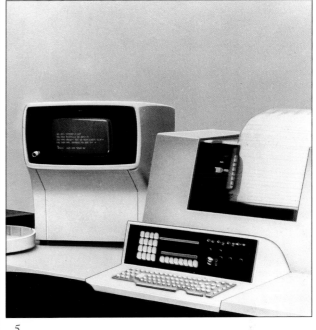

5

4 *The age-old fountain pen was dead and the ballpoint offered a new sophisticated look. Because they worked in airless and weightless conditions, these new designs were known as "spacepens". This is an updated version of a sixties classic.*

5 *By 1969, IBM had launched their System 3, which was designed to control a group of terminals in an "on-line work station environment". In other words, office computers could at last be linked into a network.*

6 *For the ordinary secretary the most important innovation was the IBM "golf-ball" typewriter.*

6

4

AIRCRAFT

1 The period saw the beginning of mass air travel. The VC10 was one of the first planes to provide regular service on the North Atlantic – the all-important route between London and New York.

2 Air transport in the sixties seems luxurious by today's standards. The seats and aisles were wide. In the early years of the decade, though, air travel was only for the few.

3 Britain's TSR2 prototype ultra-low-level nuclear bomber. It was cancelled, ostensibly because of excessive costs. However, the rumour was that it was not possible to get the advanced terrain-following radar to work.

4 The Vickers Vanguard soon found itself outdated, for propeller-driven planes could not compete with modern jetliners. And it was laughably small compared with the 747 Jumbo jet.

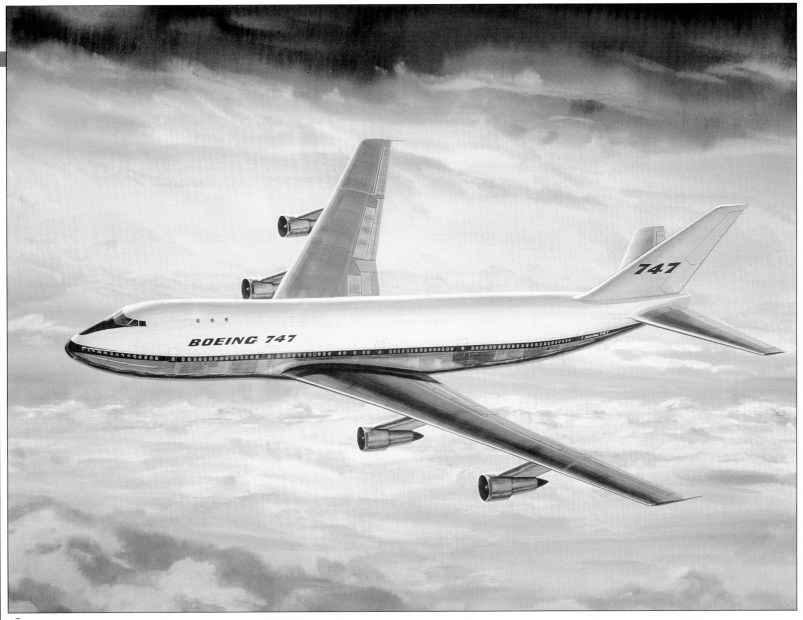

5

5 *In the sixties, people could scarcely believe that an aircraft the size of the Boeing 747 could fly. But its capacity meant that nearly everyone could now fly at an affordable price.*

6 *The Anglo-French Concorde brought supersonic air travel to those who could afford it. Its sonic boom, unacceptable over land, and its fuel capacity, which does not allow it to fly the Pacific without refuelling, made mass travel by Concorde a temporary dead-end.*

6

CARS AND MOTORBIKES

1

2

3

1 *The British sports car – the E-type Jaguar, the MGB, the Triumph Spitfire – had held sway. But America struck back with the Corvette Sting Ray. Young, fun, fast cars, they were nevertheless*

unacceptable by the early seventies. Petrol prices ruled out purely leisure motoring and soft-tops were too vulnerable to growing urban crime.

2 *British and American motorbikes lost their ascendancy, too. The Japanese came up with a new generation of superbikes – the first was Honda's CB750.*

3 *A close-up of Honda's CB750, the first Japanese four-cylinder machine. No Western manufacturer could make such a powerful machine without excessive weight.*

4 *The epitome of phallic machinery, the E-type Jaguar was the decade's ultimate sports car. This is the GT fixed-head coupé version. But if you were really trendy, you had a "rag top".*

5 *The Mini was the trendy vehicle of the sixties – but if you really wanted to win friends and influence people, you needed a Mini-Moke. This was the kit version, turning the basic car into a stripped-down jeep.*

6 *The 1960s Austin Rover – a Mini plus "badge" engineering. In class-bound Britain, if you were young, there was no real choice but the democratic vehicle of the day.*

4

WAR MACHINES

1

2

3

1 *The F-111 first saw conflict over Vietnam. This version – the F-111F – carried a laser target designation system and located laser-guided bombs.*

2 *Despite President Kennedy's policy of small "surrogate" wars between the superpowers, there was still much emphasis on intercontinental ballistic missiles. Here the American Poseidon missile, launched from a Lafayette-class nuclear submarine, is put through its paces.*

3 *The Russians were not afraid of showing off their strength. Every May Day they paraded their missiles through Moscow's Red Square.*

4 *Bell Helicopter's Huey – the "chopper" that made the Vietnam war possible. It evacuated the dead and injured, dropped assault troops and, armed with heavy guns and rockets, acted as a flying firebase.*

5 *The M16 Armalite automatic rifle was issued first to ground troops fighting in the Vietnam war. Light and made largely from plastic, it was designed to be self-cleaning. In the field, this was far from the case.*

4

5

HOUSEHOLD GADGETS

1 *The fitted kitchen was a sixties innovation and even the new tower blocks took notice of this fashion. In Europe, dishwashers and cookers were still not streamlined but bulky and old-fashioned. However, for the first time, the refrigerator became a necessity.*

2 *Both girls and boys had to dry and style their long hair. Ronson, Braun and other manufacturers came up with small, portable units with jet, comb, curl and hood attachments. The Ronson Courier shown here could be slung over the shoulder so that you could walk about while drying your hair.*

3 *The sixties saw the spread of parquet flooring, and Hoover developed new ways of polishing it, as well as of vacuum-cleaning carpets. This Hoover electric floor polisher dates from 1966.*

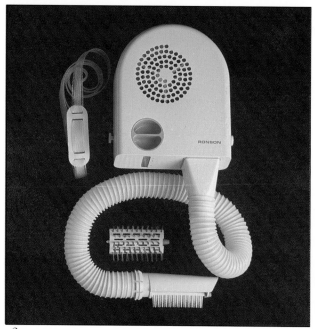

4 *Plastic was still a relatively new and unexploited material. There was something young about it, especially when used for purposes traditionally reserved for china and precious metal. Stackable plastic crockery and disposable plastic cutlery were the younger generation's way of cocking a snook at the pretensions of their elders and betters.*

5 *The decade changed life at home in other ways too. The consumer boom of the fifties in America spread to Europe and the rest of the world. Europeans who formerly had servants had to fend for themselves and the electric iron, among other devices, became a blessing.*

6 *The kitchen turned into a mini-factory. Machines were developed to mix, blend, squeeze, beat, fold and do anything else that once would have been done by hand. This was a revolution for the ordinary housewife. But, for the new liberated generation of young women, it did little to make life in the kitchen more attractive.*

5

6

RADIO, TV, HI-FI

1

2

3

1 *The "tranny" was one of the great symbols of the sixties. It was small – thanks to the Japanese – cheap enough to be bought by the young, easily transportable, blared the new music and annoyed the hell out of the older generation.*

2 *Sony developed the portable TV. It was little more than a gimmick to be shown off on posh picnics. The technology that made it feasible, though, led to many later developments.*

3 *Music was all-important. Manufacturers rushed to produce portable record players. Then stereo came along and they had to start again.*

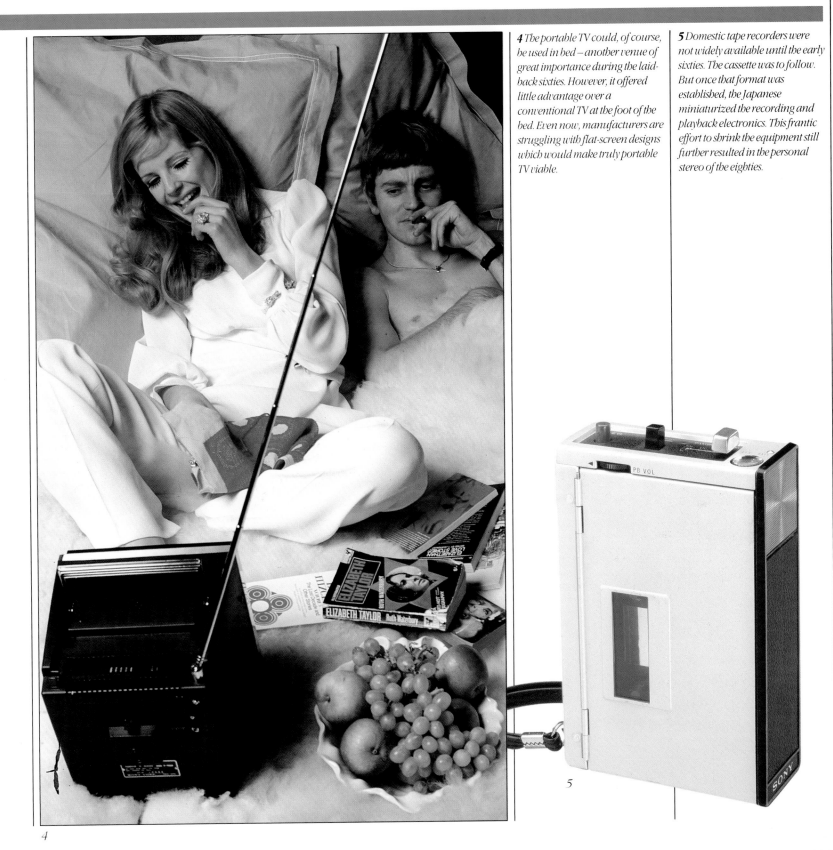

4 The portable TV could, of course, be used in bed – another venue of great importance during the laid-back sixties. However, it offered little advantage over a conventional TV at the foot of the bed. Even now, manufacturers are struggling with flat-screen designs which would make truly portable TV viable.

5 Domestic tape recorders were not widely available until the early sixties. The cassette was to follow. But once that format was established, the Japanese miniaturized the recording and playback electronics. This frantic effort to shrink the equipment still further resulted in the personal stereo of the eighties.

4

5

Classic design from this decade.

CHAPTER · FIVE

THE PAD
AND
OTHER
HABITATS

INTRODUCTION

When the sixties dawned, one thing seemed sacred. The functionalism that the Bauhaus and the Modernist pioneers had given to the world in the 1930s was not up for grabs. In architecture and design, form must follow function. There was no room for decoration, disposability or frivolity. The purism of the new age allowed no sense of humour.

In 1955, Florence Knoll had put back into production the classic Bauhaus furniture designs of the pre-war Modernists, notably Mies van de Rohe and Marcel Breuer, and there was a ready market for them. Doyen of the New Journalism of the sixties, Tom Wolfe, noted that at that time every young architect's walk-up apartment contained a coarse-grained sisal rug, a couch which was a single mattress supported by bricks and covered with a piece of monk's cloth, a clamp-on heat lamp with half-globe aluminium reflectors and a Mies van der Rohe "Barcelona" chair.

Although everything else was make-shift and "functional", the leather and stainless steel "workers'" chair designed for the 1929 Barcelona Exposition may have been functionalist but it was not at all functional. It cost a staggering $550. Mies van der Rohe used them in pairs. Wolfe says that the young architects were always scraping by to save up for the second one.

The discomforts of style

Worse though, in this haven of functionalism, was being invited to dinner. Wolfe says that Mies van der Rohe's ubiquitous S-shaped, tubular-steel, cane-bottomed chairs were so functional that by the time the main course had arrived, at least one guest had been pitched face-first into the lobster bisque.

Though pure Modernism had also found a new home at furniture-makers Hille in Britain and E. Kold Christensen in Denmark, it was the Italians who took Modernist ideas and gave them style. Even the most conventional of the Italian designers felt free to put aside the pure dogma that Germany's Hochschule für Gestaltung sought to impose. They experimented with new materials, always adding a certain Italian panache to whatever they produced. The furniture of Cassina, Tecno

1 White, symbolizing innocence, purity and youth, was the colour of the closing years of the decade. However, the white approach was not as rigorous as it was to become later. In the seventies, the white room would become such an icon for architects that they would try to get rid of any coloured trappings in the home. In the sixties, though, white was just a part of the "anything goes" approach, and, in general, the more eclectic the better. This room has Greek urns, rush matting, white walls, curtains and sofa – the other sofa is green – and a glass table. Everything was trendy, yet relaxed.

1

and Kartell, and the lights produced by Flos and Artemide, were practical yet chic.

More radical groups like Archizoom and Superstudio, founded in Florence in 1966, saw that one of the primary duties of the designer was to provide stimulation. American Pop had arrived in Italy at the Venice Biennale of 1964 and the designer Ettore Sottsass popularized the more subversive notions of British Pop after a trip to London in 1966. These radicals – who included Cesare Casati, Emanuele Ponzio, Piero Giladi and Joe Colombo – began producing provocative, dramatic, iconoclastic designs which even drew on the excesses of Dada. However radical their designs were though, they were never vulgar, never less than chic.

Debunking functionalism

In Britain, the design theorist Reyner Banham drew attention to the great failure of functionalism. The functionalists had maintained that a chair, say, was for sitting on – and that function fixed its form. Banham pointed out that a chair had other uses. "Chairs are simply detached

2 This way-out bathroom was designed by David Mlinaric for his own home. The psychedelic wallpaper by John Whiteley would alone give you a lift, while the palms would make you feel ecological. But if you were seriously into the sixties fad for recreational drugs, this bathroom would hardly have made you start the day feeling well.

3 Stark early-sixties interior design. The picture is uncompromisingly Modernist. The dressing-table chair is collapsible, the walls white, the sitting-room chairs moulded, the sofa boxed. And the coffee table is, of course, topped with glass.

3

2

units of a commonwealth of horizontal surfaces on which any number of objects, including the human fundament, can be parked," he said. In other words, you can put your feet on them, stand on them to change a light bulb, rest a TV dinner on them, put plants, books and other objects on them, even do your ironing on them if you have not got an ironing board.

Banham's remarks sounded almost flippant when he first made them but other designers took notice. Roger Dean produced his soft, formless "Sea Urchin" chair in 1967. Soon bean bags and "sag bags" containing countless plastic or expanded polystyrene beads that were supposed to mould themselves to the shape of the body, began to take over from the formal chair. The Italian design team of Gatti, Paolini and Teodoro came up with a chic version called "Sacco".

By the time the hippies arrived, chairs had gone out of fashion altogether. Scatter cushions were thrown around the floor for the laid-back flower children to loll on. Some trace this trend back to the film *Barbarella,* where Jane Fonda's spaceship was furnished in fur-covered surfaces that were hard enough to walk on but soft enough to lie on. The radical design group Archigram proposed such "interior landscapes", and these saw the light of day in Roger Dean's design for the club Upstairs at Ronnie Scott's in London. This try-out venue for up-and-coming bands was too small for conventional furniture, so Dean designed tiered structures of high-density polythene. These were soft enough to sit on and lean against, and, as they were covered with a durable carpet fabric, you could also clamber over them with impunity.

The triumph of the new

Britain had seen Modernism triumph in the shape of Robin Day's stackable "Polyprop" chair. The fitting-out of the new cruise-liner the QE2 gave Modernist British designers an international forum. Fitted "modular" kitchens and built-in wardrobes and cupboards in new homes also gave functionalists a field day.

But among young designers, another mood was afoot. In the fast-moving sixties young people did not want stark, severe, well-designed furniture that would last a lifetime. They wanted furniture that moved with the times, which was as disposable as fashion and could be changed as easily as your lifestyle. In 1964 Peter Murdoch developed the paper chair. Covered in bright Pop Art and Op Art designs, they were laminated and washable and would last between three and six months. The International Paper Corporation in America found they could stamp them out of a printed sheet – ready pressed and scored – one a second for a few cents each. Storage and transportation were cheap too. Eight hundred paper chairs stacked only 4ft (1.25m) high. The chairs were sold flat – the customer simply folded them into shape at home. The price? Even

1

when they were re-exported back to England they cost only 30s. (£1.50).

Bernard Holloway designed the Tomtom range of strong cardboard furniture, based on a series of large cardboard tubes. Chairs sold for £2 and a 54-inch (140cm) table for £6 17s 6d (£6.75). David Bartlett's polythene laminated fibreboard chair, known as the Tab – again sold flat, to be folded and assembled by the customer – sold for 45s. (£2.25).

Knockdown living

Although people quickly tired of paper, the idea of furniture bought flat and assembled at home – so-called "knockdown" furniture – caught on. In 1965, Max Clendinning came up with the Maxima range. There were 25 standard parts – sheets of brightly painted plywood – which could be bolted together in nearly 300 different ways to make chairs, tables or wall-hung units.

Carol Russell even designed a range of furniture that could be cut from a single sheet of plywood and which, when not in use, could be folded and hung on the wall as a piece of instant abstract art.

In 1964, British pop designers Cedric Price and Arthur Quarmby developed inflatable furniture, but this did not become generally available until 1967 with the transparent Blow Chair designed by Scolari, Lomazzi, d'Urbino and de Pas in Italy. Quasar Khanh produced chairs and a

1 A capsule kitchen on show at London's Design Centre in 1968. This approach capitalized on the advent of moulded synthetic materials. It was a logical progression for the fully fitted kitchen but, somehow, people did not take to this over-organized approach. There have to be some chance elements in any room, something to suit the individual. Many of the architectural and design ideas failed because ordinary people did not want to live in rooms that resembled factories or laboratories.

2 Stripped pine made its first appearance during the sixties. It was proletarian, as were exposed bricks and beams. A little of the old in the clock, a little of the new in the chair – the taste of the period embraced it all.

sofa in transparent or coloured PVC elements which could be filled with air or coloured water. The elements were connected by metal rings. Khanh later took inflatables a stage further when he designed an inflatable room and a transparent car.

In Britain Paul Woods created a similar range of inflatable furniture where the elements were connected with nylon nuts and bolts. Incadinc produced the Air Chair. Pakamac made a translucent chair and matching stool. And X-Lon produced a range of inflatable pop cushions.

Down-to-earth drawbacks

Inflatables had one drawback though: they were vulnerable to puncturing by sharp objects and lighted cigarette ends. They were therefore sold with a repair kit comprising PVC patches and glue. Worse, in some designs the seams ruptured easily, a problem the manufacturers never fully overcame.

Despite their remarkably low price – less than a third of the price of a similar item of conventional furniture – inflatables never really caught on. The public did not see them as proper furniture. As the sixties drew to a close and people began to become more conscious of the environment, the wanton expendability of paper, cardboard and blow-up furniture seemed almost immoral. Customers also became more suspicious of manufacturers and retailers. And items which had to be erected at home were seen as a convenience for the manufacturer and seller, rather than for the consumer.

Wallpaper and textile design were influenced by Op Art. And as the race to put a man on the moon hotted up towards the end of the sixties, space-age furniture in tubular steel, white and silver, came in, giving thirties Modernism another chance to re-assert itself. Nostalgia for the thirties, for the Victorian era, and even for some idealized rural past became the prevailing mood of the time. Young people began to buy Victorian and Edwardian furniture in junk shops and thrift stores, and the wallpaper patterns of William Morris and C.F.A. Voysey went back into production.

A ragbag of styles

Psychedelia – with its Art Nouveau motifs – also had its effect on wallpaper design, but the true hippy pad was decorated with an extraordinary eclectic mix of objets trouvés – the sort of things that might be found in the tent of an Arab sheikh who had pitched camp in London's Portobello Road.

But while hippies crashed out on heaps of scatter cushions, a mind-boggling mixture of Neo-Bauhaus tubular-steel furniture, exotic hand-woven rugs and stark stripped-pine tables and benches began to find its way into the homes of the middle classes.

3 The sixties pad was somewhere to relax, even if it meant lying on the floor or sprawling on the sofa. The crash pad was not far away.

4 This house, designed by Ralf Erskine in Sweden in 1966, is severe and functional in the extreme – but it still has the elements of fun that were also characteristic of the time.

2

3

4

INSPIRATIONS

1

3

2

1 *Ethnic influences began in the sixties. Hippies, junkies, homosexuals and others who took the Marrakesh trail brought back pots to stand on their patios and rugs to hang on their walls.*

4 *Tubular steel, used here by the Dutch functionalist architect Mart Stam, came back into fashion.*

5 *Mies van der Rohe's famous 1929 Barcelona chair came back into production in the sixties and was much emulated.*

6 *Art Deco flaunted the modern for its own sake as did the sixties: everything old belonged on the scrap heap, although eclecticism made borrowing from the thirties respectable.*

7 *Life, youth decided, should ape art – not the other way round – and the influence of film, theatre and music found its way into fashion and interior design. Life should be lived in a movie set.*

4

6

5

2 *The Third World certainly had a great influence on interior design in the late sixties. Many a hippy's crash pad ended up looking like this after a week or so of parties.*

3 *This cotton carpet design for a nursery by Benita Otte at the Bauhaus in 1923 became very popular in the sixties. Such bold designs were found hanging on walls everywhere.*

7

MODERNISM

1 The egg shape was a perfect symbol for the period. It was simple, innocent and easy to form in plastic. It was both trendy and perfect for meditation. Just pull your legs up into the shell, adopt the lotus position and say "Om". The colour supplement was new to British newspapers in the sixties too. The shell's tubular steel-support and simplicity of form would not have been out of place in the thirties. Mod owed much to Modernism.

2 These S-shaped chairs with wicker seats and backs are versions of the classic Mart Stam S33 tubular-steel chair designed in 1926. The slab-topped table, the imitation bottle-glass partition and the bare-block, unplastered walls are all pure thirties Modernism. The paper-globe lampshade is still on sale today.

2

1

3

3 *Oliver Morgue's classic 1963 chaise longue – perfect for Freudian analysis, another hangover from the 1930s that found new life in the sixties. Its form perfectly fits its function, with absolutely no frills. But it was a little too comfortable to get the full Bauhaus seal of approval.*

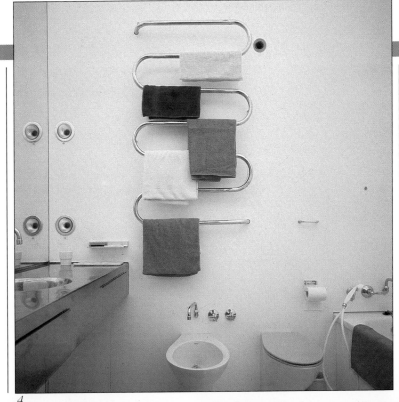

6

4

4 *The bathroom of a house in Wimbledon, London, designed by Su and Richard Rogers. The new ease of foreign travel helped bring the bidet, and the shower, to Britain. The heated towel rail was new, too. But the circular sink, hollowed seamlessly from the bathroom surface, the recessed lighting, the single-spout hot and cold tap, and the stark, cramped finish all echo the thirties.*

5 *The severity of these moulded plywood dining-room chairs, designed for the senior common room at Oxford's new St Catherine's College, is pure Modernism.*

6 *A stern thirties look was perfect for the refurbishment of the QE2. This restaurant chair was designed by Robert Heritage for Race Furniture. The colours are classic sixties, though.*

5

NEW MATERIALS

1 *Although artificiality was a Mod virtue, to pander to older, more conservative customers some manufacturers of new materials tried to imitate nature. Here Formica's "Nubian" plastic laminate tries hard to look like wood.*

2 *Plastic has its own natural springiness and the designers of far-out furniture attempted to exploit the new material's characteristics. Some brave efforts drew the applause of the inner circle of taste, but found little house room.*

1

3 *A new material in the world of furniture, plastic was clean, bright and functional. It was also cheap and easy to form. And if the design was stackable, it made furniture perfect for institutional use.*

2

3

5 Acrylic was another novel material in the brave new world of sixties furniture. It worked well for tables, but for chairs it proved harsh and uncomfortable.

6 Until the sixties, no one had thought of using paper to make furniture. But this was the age of disposability. Peter Murdoch's disposable paper chair of 1964 for children was followed in 1966 by David Bartlett's adult version, the Tab.

5

4

4 One of the most innovative use of new materials was the plastic "inflatable". The Blow Chair – designed by Scolari, Lomazzi, D'Urbino and De Pas in 1967 – was one of the most successful. Some people filled them with water and put tropical fish in, but these quickly suffocated. Inflatables were comfortable and offered certain erotic possibilities – all important in the newly liberated sixties. But they could be sweaty.

6

REVIVALISM

1

1 Any period would do: the elegance of Regency, brass bedsteads, electrified oil lamps, old prints and other antique knick-knacks, all were mixed and matched.

2 The old-fashioned uniforms that were so much in vogue were the clue. The British were feeling bullish, and revelling in nostalgia for the time they ruled the world. Phonographs, antique furniture and coronation plates – Queen Victoria's – hanging on the wall created the right atmosphere, provided they were treated with the appropriate healthy, democratic disrespect.

2

3

3 The twenties would do just as well as any other source era for the eclectic sixties. Feather boas, two-tone shoes and wicker chairs, white suits and curtains, white dogs and walls, Art Nouveau and Art Deco – all found new life in the clothes and interior design of Biba. But the secret was not to try to look authentic. The sixties had its own style – it may have borrowed, and plagiarized shamelessly, but it never tried to be any other period.

4 The gingerbread house out of Count Dracula. *Fantasy was reality. Rooms were filmsets in which you played out your life. The decor was borrowed from other periods, other cultures – and most of all from the movies. It was important to look theatrical and, if possible, surreal.* Alice in Wonderland *would not be out of place here. Nor would the Wicked Witch of the East.*

4

PSYCHEDELIA

1 *Kids always wanted to sit on the floor, even before psychedelia came along. It was cool, relaxed. Bean bags were good, but a huge psychedelic mattress was better. No trendy crashpad was complete without one. Too much drink or drugs and you did not have to move.*

2 *Even your bathroom could be psychedelic. But if you could not get around to decorating it, it was nice to make heady plans. The painting of the dream bathroom could be enough.*

3 *Bamboo lent itself well to painted exaggeration – as well as being light, cheap and practical. The blue chair, for instance, with its Somerset Maugham parasol, was surprisingly comfortable. The chest – its decoration inspired by an umbrella handle – has silks in oriental colours spewing from its drawers. It is topped by a bookcase in Regency style. The hallstand with town and country gear, the sturdy three-compartment magazine rack, the flower stand, the three-tier table with Victorian stuffed birds – all are obviously the work of a mind disordered by strange substances.*

4 You did not need to have experienced pot, LSD and mescalin to get into psychedelia – just as long as your interior decorator or fashion designer had. Drugs were not that widespread, though their motifs were everywhere. If your rooms were full of mind-expanding images and your dress suggested something to do with Flower Power, there was no need to take a trip. You could be groovy enough over a glass of sweet sherry. Besides, the "heads" on the streets and the hippies who really had dropped out of the material world could not afford these trappings. In the sixties, if you did not really believe any of the mystical philosophies that were being peddled wholesale, you could have it all.

4

OPEN-PLAN LIVING

1

2

3

1 *Open-plan was very popular. This house by Aldington and Craig replaced an outside wall. Who cared what the neighbours thought? Had they not ever seen someone naked before?*

2 *The patio became part of the room. The French windows in this house in Wimbledon, London, designed by Su and Richard Rogers, simply slide aside to let in the garden.*

3 *In the sixties, nothing needed to be hidden, hence sliding partition walls.*

4 *Hall, stairs, TV room, sitting room, garden, landing – try and spot where one room stops and another begins.*

4

Psychedelic graphics advertise rock 'n' roll.

CHAPTER SIX

THE WRITING ON THE WALL

"In future, everyone will be famous for fifteen minutes."

ANDY WARHOL

INTRODUCTION

The death knell was sounded – somewhat prematurely – for the print media. The guru of the TV age Marshall McLuhan predicted the imminent demise of "the Gutenberg Galaxy". He believed that the invention of print had torn humankind from its oral heritage and made it *linear*. Television, he claimed, was returning humankind to its oral tradition, receiving ideas in the form of images.

And it seemed to be true. During the sixties 163 magazines – including New York's legendary *Saturday Evening Post* – and 160 daily newspapers died in the USA. In Britain too, titles that seemed to be deeply entwined in the fabric of the nation disappeared from the news-stands. Even *The Times* of London was forced to move its small ads and put news on the front page!

A revitalized press

But those newspapers and magazines that survived changed and grew stronger. British Sunday papers added US-style colour supplements which, back then at their inception, carried strong investigative stories with a heavy pictorial content. What's more, 176 *new* daily papers were launched in the USA. And new magazines catering to sixties topics – music, hi-fi, youth fashions and, in Britain, satire – sprang up almost weekly. Maybe TV wasn't going to kill off the press after all.

In magazines, the public's idea of the romantic lead was no longer the writer but the photographer, especially the fashion photographer. As early as 1959, Antony Armstrong Jones (later Lord Snowdon) introduced his action style to *Vogue*. He made his models run, dance, kiss – anything but stand still. Visual tricks were used to make the photograph interesting in itself, rather than just an illustration of the garment.

In the early sixties when a new generation of photographers – David Bailey, Bryan Duffy, Terence Donovan – came on the scene, the garment became almost secondary. For them, the important thing was the projection of a total image. Not only did the garment have to be the latest, the most fashionable, but the model had to stand in the latest way and project the latest attitude. The whole performance had to be the thing of the moment. Duffy believed that the more on the ball you were, the quicker your images would go out of date. He aimed at a shelf-life of six weeks.

Working relationships

Alongside fashion photographers, fashion models like Twiggy became the in-est of in people. Jean Shrimpton became the symbol of swinging London through her work with David Bailey, whose pictures went to no lengths at all to conceal his involvement with his model. Rather he flaunted it. Bryan Duffy believes that Bailey was responsible for the mini-skirt. He says that Bailey would show off

1

2

Jean Shrimpton's legs even when it was inappropriate for the garment she was modelling, simply because he liked them.

In 1965, Bailey showed that his interests went beyond fashion photography when he published *Bailey's Box of Pin Ups*. This included portraits of pop stars, artists, hairstylists, top businessmen, models, other photographers, even criminals like East London's notorious Kray brothers – anyone who was being gossiped about or featured in the media at the time. Bailey's adoration of the in people was successfully sent up when the Krays were tried at London's Old Bailey in 1969 and the satirical magazine *Private Eye* used the photographer's – whom they referred to as David Old Bailey – glamorized shot of the twins on its front cover.

After 1965 though, the world became a much more serious place. The Vietnam conflict created a new generation of war photographers – Don McCullen, Tim Page, Sean Flynn – whose pictures brought the war home vividly in the American news magazines and the British glossy colour supplements.

Magazines used the new photo-litho printing techniques to produce layouts that were much more visual. The printed word was sculpted around pictures and into bubbles, tears and other novel shapes. Pictures were printed grainy, and stark sanserif type that ran to the edge of the page took print to the limit of legibility. Visual impact was all.

Targeting a readership

In 1966-7, the underground press took this trend even further. *International Times, Yarrow Roots,* and *Oz* – the prosecution of which for obscenity was one of the great legal battles of the decade – were printed in small type sizes over pictures reproduced in psychedelic colours – pink on orange, for example. The idea seemed to be that no one straight or over 30 should read them.

Even further downmarket were the leaflets. In the sixties, you could buy a new hand-cranked mimeograph for $300 or a second-hand one for $60. A used offset press cost $300. With paper at $1 for a thousand sheets, student groups, underground event organizers, anti-war groups, hippies, socialists and just plain nutcases could run off leaflets by the thousand and hand them out to passers-by on the streets.

One of the archetypal images of the 1960s was the nude – especially the female nude. Naked women turned up everywhere, in the theatre, in the cinema, in newspapers, in advertisements and on TV – in Britain at least. A nude woman even appeared in an advertisement in *The Times* of London. The soft-porn magazine *Playboy* stopped being furtive and began to see itself as being in the vanguard of the sexual revolution. Circulation took off in a way that was unprecedented. *Mayfair, Penthouse* and,

1 Oz magazine led where few dared follow. Their anarchic mixture of pornography, incitement to revolution and drug abuse was presented with panache and an innovative use of typography and graphics that made the whole explosive mixture incomprehensible. In their school kids' issue, they turned the editorial content of the magazine over to a bunch of school kids, and then got busted for obscenity.

2 Jean Shrimpton – along with Twiggy – was the face of fashion in the sixties. David Bailey's obsession with her – and especially with her legs – reduced the model's clothes to irrelevance.

3 Playboy was at the radical cutting edge of the sexual revolution in the sixties. Publisher and long-time editor Hugh Heffner still claims to have invented women's liberation.

3

eventually, *Screw* followed it into the marketplace.

The covers of Penguin books were revamped in the sixties. During the previous decade a decision had been made to eschew pictorial covers, which Penguin linked to lurid American mass-market paperbacks. But in 1961, under the art-editorship of Germano Facetti, strong visual images were introduced, initially on Penguin's crime series. The cover grid designed by Romek Marber was so flexible that subtle variations were possible across the company's lists, each identified with a distinct colour and style. Young graphic designer and illustrator Alan Aldridge began introducing sex, irony, humour and fantasy, Pop style. But in 1967 Penguin publisher Allen Lane felt that this gimmickry had gone far enough. A book is not a tin of beans, he said. Aldridge went on to produce *The Beatles' Illustrated Lyrics* in 1969, an anthology of Pop graphics which included the work of 45 British and American illustrators and photographers.

Pop Art images cropped up everywhere. Union Jacks, the Stars and Stripes, targets and Op Art patterns appeared on mugs, bags, patches and tee-shirts. Mary Quant used the style of Batman on the instruction leaflet that came with her cosmetics. Lee Cooper even reproduced a Lichtenstein painting, *Pistol*, on a tee-shirt, without the painter's permission. Tee-shirts also featured pop stars and cult figures like the revolutionary leader Che Guevara.

Psychedelia surfaced in advertisements and, particularly on posters advertising pop concerts. Wes Wilson pioneered the style in 1967 with his concert posters for the Filmore Auditorium, in San Francisco. In London, Weymouth and English produced psychedelic graphics – for the Who, among others – under the name Hapshash and the Coloured Coat. They also produced a series of huge psychedelic murals for the front of the hip boutique Granny Takes a Trip in the Kings Road. John Lennon had his Rolls Royce customized with psychedelic squiggles and Pop artist Alexander Calder even came up with a psychedelic livery for Braniff International's fleet of passenger jets. The psychedelic fad did not last long, though. Psychedelic images were so brilliant and so jarring that people were soon complaining of retinal overload.

Cultural pirates

The whole of the sixties can be seen as a search for stimulation, which made it a very eclectic time. Art Nouveau and Art Deco styles, among others, were copied unashamedly. This can be seen most clearly in the evolution of Biba, Barbara Hulanicki's boutique which turned superstore in 1969. The styles of Aubrey Beardsley, images of the film stars of the twenties and thirties, Victoriana, the religious imagery of the East – everything seemed a source ripe for plundering.

Album sales soared during the sixties and the style of

1 There is nothing radical about the depiction of the Beatles here – except that their hair was getting a bit long for 1966 – but the lettering of Rubber Soul *is revolutionary. This squidgy calligraphy only really came into its own with the aerosol can and subway trains in the eighties.*

2 If it had the name Beatles on it, it would sell. As the foremost poets of their day and tied into an older tradition – with Victorian lightweights such as Lewis Carroll and Edward Lear, the Beatles were a very potent selling device.

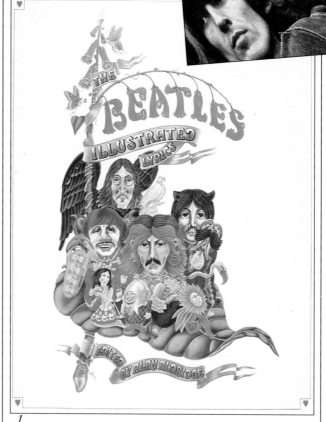

1

3 Poster for a San Francisco rock concert. Presented by Bill Graham, the line-up promised the Who and Loading Zone.

their covers was set, naturally, by the Beatles. The sleeve of the first album *Please Please Me*, released in April 1963, was a triumph of the banal, showing the Fab Four looking down from the balcony of Parlophone's headquarters, with the title in muddled multi-coloured type. Their second, *With the Beatles* (called *Meet the Beatles* in the USA), which came out in November 1963, used a grainy black and white shot by the fashion photographer Robert Freeman, which showed their heads starkly sidelit and floating on a black background. David Bailey used much the same style on the Rolling Stones' second album.

The cover of the Beatles' third album *A Hard Day's*

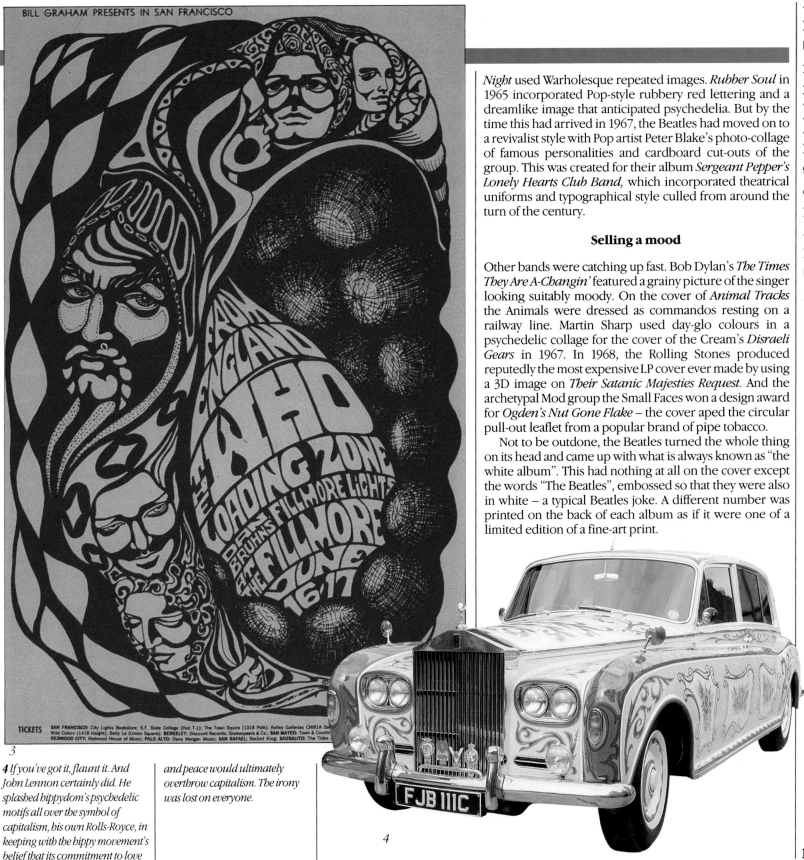

BILL GRAHAM PRESENTS IN SAN FRANCISCO

Night used Warholesque repeated images. *Rubber Soul* in 1965 incorporated Pop-style rubbery red lettering and a dreamlike image that anticipated psychedelia. But by the time this had arrived in 1967, the Beatles had moved on to a revivalist style with Pop artist Peter Blake's photo-collage of famous personalities and cardboard cut-outs of the group. This was created for their album *Sergeant Pepper's Lonely Hearts Club Band,* which incorporated theatrical uniforms and typographical style culled from around the turn of the century.

Selling a mood

Other bands were catching up fast. Bob Dylan's *The Times They Are A-Changin'* featured a grainy picture of the singer looking suitably moody. On the cover of *Animal Tracks* the Animals were dressed as commandos resting on a railway line. Martin Sharp used day-glo colours in a psychedelic collage for the cover of the Cream's *Disraeli Gears* in 1967. In 1968, the Rolling Stones produced reputedly the most expensive LP cover ever made by using a 3D image on *Their Satanic Majesties Request*. And the archetypal Mod group the Small Faces won a design award for *Ogden's Nut Gone Flake* – the cover aped the circular pull-out leaflet from a popular brand of pipe tobacco.

Not to be outdone, the Beatles turned the whole thing on its head and came up with what is always known as "the white album". This had nothing at all on the cover except the words "The Beatles", embossed so that they were also in white – a typical Beatles joke. A different number was printed on the back of each album as if it were one of a limited edition of a fine-art print.

3

4 If you've got it, flaunt it. And John Lennon certainly did. He splashed hippydom's psychedelic motifs all over the symbol of capitalism, his own Rolls-Royce, in keeping with the hippy movement's belief that its commitment to love and peace would ultimately overthrow capitalism. The irony was lost on everyone.

4

TICKETS SAN FRANCISCO: City Lights Bookstore; S.F. State College (Hut T-1); The Town Squire (1318 Polk); Kelley Galleries (3681A ...); Wild Colors (1418 Haight); Bally Lo (Union Square); BERKELEY: Discount Records; Shakespeare & Co.; SAN MATEO: Town & Country; REDWOOD CITY: Redwood House of Music; PALO ALTO: Dana Morgan Music; SAN RAFAEL: Record King; SAUSALITO: The Tides ...

INSPIRATIONS

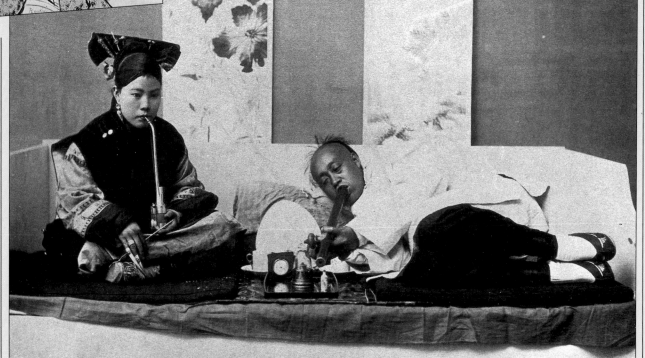

1 *Aubrey Beardsley's strong graphic sense and his use of divinely decadent images made him a popular model in the sixties, especially after the exhibition of his work in London in the summer of 1966.*

2 *Toulouse-Lautrec, with his decadent lifestyle, was another hero of the sixties. Reprints of his posters were popular.*

3 *The bold propaganda of this 1925 poster by Alexander Rodchenko for the Lengiz publishing house was one of the models for the agitprop movement that surrounded the student unrest of 1968.*

4 *Drugs, of course, were a major influence in all aspects of life in the sixties. East finally met West. And East won. The louche habits of the orient were brought back by young people who had followed the hippy trail and by veterans of the Vietnam war who had learnt the habit of smoking opium.*

5 *The simple direct style of advertising posters for the London Underground and the various railway companies in the twenties had its place too in directing sixties' design. The austere styles of the forties and fifties were out.*

5

7

6 *The nightmare world of modernism portrayed in* Metropolis *had already come true. In the sixties. people believed that the human race had come through it, into a blissful new utopia. The nightmare images were now used with faint nostalgia.*

7 *And behind it all was the waste of the Vietnam war. This was one of the first pictures of the fifties to come through the wire services. It shocked the world. Soon TV pictures of human life being bombed, burnt and blown apart became regular fodder for the nightly TV news. And the real-life nightmare of the unwinnable war seeped into the American psyche.*

8

8 *Letraset arrived in the sixties. It brought hundreds of typefaces – old and new – within the reach of every graphic designer. The new photolithographic printing techniques meant that, for the first time, designers could make up their own headlines and present them as camera-ready artwork to the printers.*

6

129

FASHION AND CELEBRITY PHOTOGRAPHY

1

3

2

4

1 *Third-world philosophies may have been in – and their influences in fashion were crucial but it is doubtful that this outfit was, as billed, a hit in the harem.*

2 *The great thing about the period was that no style was out of place. This black Dior hat was modelled by Baroness von Thyssen and photographed by Cecil Beaton.*

3 *Black and white came together in Op Art at least. Or in zebra-striped chiffon by Jane and Jane at Chanelle, modelled by Diana Ross, then lead singer with the Supremes.*

4 *Cecil Beaton was even at home photographing Flower Power – or at least the mainstream reflection of it. This Organza outfit is posh and rich. All the aristocratic virtues of the thirties are on display.*

5 *Whatever Twiggy wore was the thing. Because of her, textured tights and heavy jewellery took off. The same accessories could look square on the wrong person. But on some young and fashionably thin model, anything would look trendy.*

6 *The actor Terence Stamp was another "face". Whatever he wore, whatever he did, wherever he went, was "in". A black velvet suit, in a tight Italian Mod fit, a psychedelic cravat, pre-designer stubble and a thirties gangster's slouch hat may be a mish-mash of styles, but in the sixties the attitude was: if it feels good, do it.*

5

6

WAR PHOTOGRAPHY

1 *In 1965, the US Marines waded ashore at Da Nang and the Vietnam war had started. Photographers like Britain's Tim Page were there to capture it. They carried with them the styles hammered out by the new generation of rock 'n' roll magazine photographers like David Bailey.*

2 *Don McCullen employed a more traditional style that had its origins in the Second World War.*

3 *Pictures by both the rock 'n' rollers and the traditionalists were used – and in each case their pictures neatly supported the point of view of the reader.*

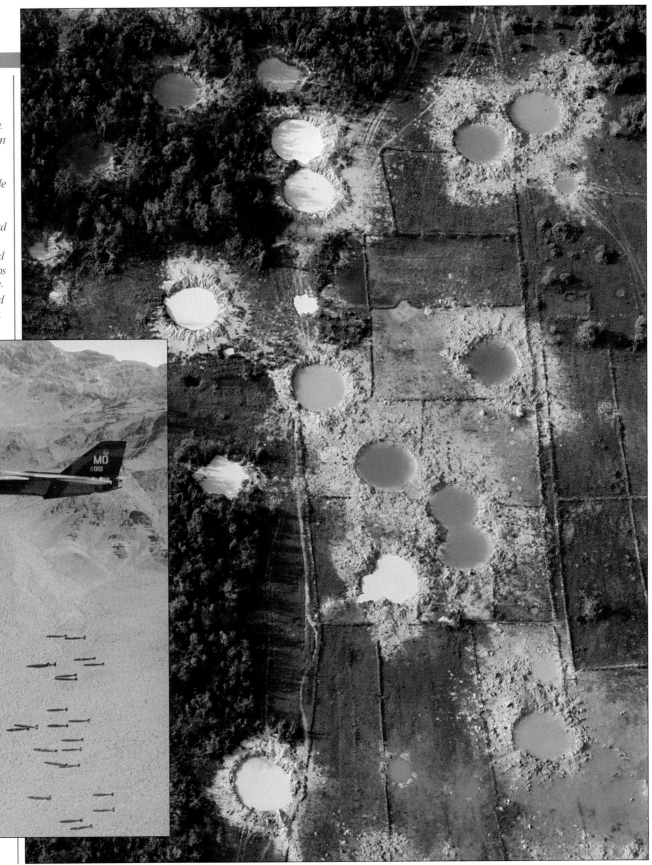

4 *The F-111 first saw action over Vietnam. It was the state-of-the-art fighter bomber. The Communists wanted one – badly. They got six. F-111s flew high when they took off, then hugged the ground with their terrain-following radar. That flight profile made them easy to spot.*

5 *The B-52 was not new, but it had a special significance in the Vietnam war. B-52s flew high and dropped millions of tons of bombs over North Vietnam, Communist-controlled areas in the South and the supply routes in neutral Laos.*

4

5

MAGAZINE DESIGN

1 Nova *was one of the most visually inventive magazines of the period. It claimed to be "A new kind of magazine for a new kind of woman".*

1

2 *American-style colour magazines became part of British Sunday newspapers. The papers took some time to shake off the American influence.*

3 *Inventive page layout became part of the new look of the sixties. Style was all-important. The new photographic style was stagy and dramatic. Its effect was heightened by the use of lots of white space. Words were still very important though.*

3

Nothing colours the public's view of the police (or anything else for that matter) quite so effectively as personal experience. The man who has had his car towed away while lingering overlong with his after-lunch brandy and then goes home to watch a TV documentary filled with stories of corrupt cops and unlawful beatings will probably be in a more likely frame of mind to accept what he sees than he would have been if a patient, smiling bobby had sought him out in the restaurant and politely asked him to do the rest of mankind a favour by moving his car. On the other hand, the parent whose straying toddler has just been returned home by an avuncular patrol man will almost certainly be in the mood to reject the programme as a wicked slander against a fine body of men toiling against bitter odds.

The anti-H-Bomb demonstrator who has been unceremoniously lifted from the Whitehall pavement and dumped in the back of a Black Maria will not need much convincing that the police are the reactionary agents of a reactionary state. Those who share the view of an American poster which I saw on tele-news recently, that all pacifists are 'Commies, cowards and queers,' will see the same harassed policemen as the unbiased guardians of decency, law and order, the royal corgis and the Marylebone Cricket Club.

Our class attitudes and social backgrounds also influence our attitude to the police. The cockney youngster ejected into the street after running on to the pitch at Chelsea football ground will probably go through life thinking of the police as 'them' the uniformed expression of the mysterious power whose will it is to see that people who break impossible rules shall never have their cake and eat it. Those who have eaten the cake, and ordered more, will not find it necessary to inquire too closely into the methods used to make sure that the deliveries shall go on uninterrupted.

In short: the public is human too.

But the public's view of the police is a fleeting one. Apart from other policemen there is only one section of the public that gets a long-term view of the police – their wives. So I have been talking to them.

During the last election, Mr Edward du Cann said that men tend to become like their dogs. With at least equal truth, often think like their husbands. So on the face of it proposition seemed reasonable enough: in what attitudes policemen have, the basic phil that inspires them, by talking to their wives. In journalism things rarely turn out exactly are planned. If they did there would ulcers around.

Policemen choose their career. Policemen don't choose to marry policemen. They marry the man they love, or – for the unromantic – the man who asks them. Being a policeman may or may not be a life vocation; it may be just another way of earning a living. Being a policeman's wife is simply to be married – to a policeman.

It is not my intention to generalise from the particular. The wives to whom I spoke were chosen at random together, they are probably fairly typical as such. They are tive ind...

Ask th... police... be tha... Yet s... to w... aged... in th... The... sub... ca... ho... tak... M...

at Scotland Yard. Yet over the years she has found herself more and more taking the side of the police in arguments with her friends. Not so long ago she had a 'fantastic, idiotic row' with a close friend because she hit back at criticisms the woman and her husband made of the police.

'I told John about it and he was terribly moved. It the first time I had struck back for the police at all the time. I am becoming the next time we... ? Ninety... th trivial... s of mar... s sort of...

ex-teacher... of the uni... e station... ir home on... gaged. Th... n any of t... er pridem... ld let her... es. I'm p...

l feel the p... ty of answ... ly. You ca... but she h... to see the... nswer back... re attacked... imagine th... ir own han... ating to a... e suggestio... blm is a v... ceman wh...

t is proba... t in the p... instance, th... w-abiding... self I know... o burst int... killed a p... I really w... n that.'...

k, the polic... n't. He's ve... personal... ago, her h... olice constable, was bea...

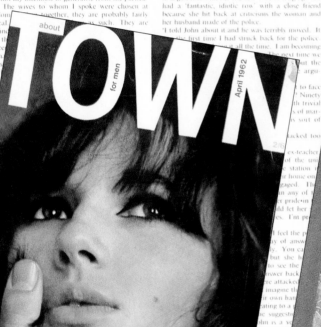

Mrs Child, then, a... policeman. One cannot imagine... as loyal little wife of the year by the powers...

59

4 *Spend, spend, spend was the motto of the time. As well as the glossy lifestyle magazine, there was a plethora of new magazines telling people where they could find a good time when they went out. Most had died by the early seventies but London's* Time Out *and New York's* Village Voice *are still going strong.*

5 *Some newspapers just soldiered on. Although* Saturday Evening Post *was laid to rest, the* New Yorker *carried on just as it had in the days of James Thurber and Dorothy Parker.*

ADVERTISING

1 *Though the connection between smoking and lung cancer had been made, there were as yet no curbs on cigarette advertising. The sexual innuendo was used innocently enough. It was the ostensibly aristocratic connotations that were flaunted.*

2 *Although women had been liberated by the Pill, sexism was still rife. Indeed the word itself did not come into common usage until the seventies. This was the age of the Playboy philosophy and its unreconstructed male chauvinism. Men wanted fast cars, sleek yachts, smooth whisky and beautiful girls.*

3 *The campaign that caused a revolution in car advertising. Black and white and lovingly dramatic, out have gone the distorted airbrush images and the admiring females. In has come realistic photography and intelligent and humorous copy.*

The famous Italian designer suggested one change.

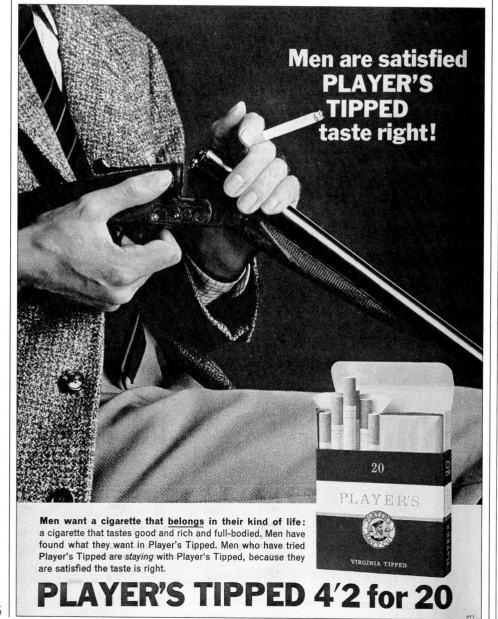

Men are satisfied PLAYER'S TIPPED taste right!

Men want a cigarette that <u>belongs</u> in their kind of life: a cigarette that tastes good and rich and full-bodied. Men have found what they want in Player's Tipped. Men who have tried Player's Tipped are *staying* with Player's Tipped, because they are satisfied the taste is right.

PLAYER'S TIPPED 4'2 for 20

HIS WOMAN   **HIS DRINK**

His . . . a world of beautiful things.
Cars, yachts, girls. But only one woman.
Like only one whisky.
Black & White is to whisky
as one all womanly woman
is to the whole wide world of girls.

'BLACK & WHITE'

1

2

3

4

Mitsouko by Guerlain

New G.E.C. Haute Cuisine—the beauty with the brains

It takes guts to charge £10 for a shaver.

5

6

4 *Women's faces and women's bodies were used to sell anything and everything in the sixties. Here, advertising a perfume, it was at least a little more appropriate. By the close of the decade, advertisements had begun to cut down on the copy lines and just let a strong image tell the story.*

5 *The housewife was still much in evidence, though. The kitchen was her province and if you wanted to sell washing machines, refrigerators or cookers you had to show a housewife proudly displaying her new purchase – or her husband's – to her best friend who is, of course, another housewife.*

6 *The electric razor was still relatively new on the European market and the feeling was that real men still used a cut-throat. So to make electric shavers more masculine, they were shown as highly mechanical – the sort of thing only a real man would understand.*

ILLUSTRATION

End Bad Breath.

1 *Uncle Sam appeared in many guises during the sixties – most of them ironic. Here Seymour Chwast makes an anti-Vietnam war statement by putting B52s and bombs where bombast usually belongs – in the mouth of America's most patriotic symbol.*

2 *Surrealism was back in this concert bill for folk-rockers the Lovin' Spoonful, illustrated by Milton Glaser.*

3 *The 1968 advertising poster of* The Different Drummer *by Peter Max used a face inspired by the 1920s. But something else was happening here, something weird, something cosmic. The psychedelic style of the Beatles' movie* Yellow Submarine *was trying to break through.*

2

1

4

4 *Swinging London looked doubly swinging when the Sunday Times illustrated its map of the city of the sixties in November 1964. The style is deliberately childlike, but the two shopping areas depicted are the most expensive in London. Illustration is by Juliet Glynn-Smith.*

5 *On this cover for the Cream's album* Disraeli Gears, *the photography of Bob Whittaker has been transmogrified by the drug-influenced Californian graphic design style of Martin Sharp. The end result is a combination of collage, swirling organic forms and day-glo colours.*

3

5

PACKAGING: THE BODY BEAUTIFUL

MARY QUANT GIVES YOU THE BARE ESSENTIALS

1

2

1 The female nude was the quintessential image of the sixties – along with flowers – much as the male nude is of the eighties. Interestingly, this make-up ad does not even bother to show the model's face.

2 Elizabeth Arden cosmetics had been around since 1910, but when the time came they did not hesitate to take on psychedelic packaging to capture a new generation of young women – and young men for that matter. Male cosmetics made their periodic reoccurrence during the decade.

3 The nude body moved out of the realm of art, through pornographic magazines and movies, into the world of advertising and packaging. Reckitt and Colman came up with a revolutionary new concept that exploited this relaxing of standards. It was a body shampoo called All Over Softly.

3

4 In the pursuit of health and the body beautiful, people turned to wholesome, natural foods like yoghurt. At the time, the media fuelled rumours that yoghurt was the magic foodstuff that allowed some citizens of the Soviet Caspian republics to live to be over 100. In fact, their birth certificates had been lost in the Revolution. Health-giving, live yoghurt was in fact too much for the modern Western consumer to take, so fruit was added. When this brand was introduced in 1963, the carton was made of waxed board, but it was changed to plastic by the end of the sixties.

5,6 To be "in" you had to be young. And to be young you had to be slim. Andy Warhol noted that, with all the slimming tablets that were taken just for kicks, many people ended the decade looking younger than when they started it. But for the more health conscious, the first mass-market slimming foods became available.

7 Women became extremely conscious of their figures. Slimming products raced to their rescue. Unicliffe Ltd of Kent, England, made Limmits Crackers – "the tastiest way to slim" – in the mid-sixties. Another English firm, Ryvita, made Starch Reduced Wheat Crispbread – "for the slimming diets in which the total intake of calories is controlled".

4

5

7

6

1 *The teenager was largely the invention of the late fifties. But in the following decade, with the baby boom, teenagers came into their own. There was full employment and teenagers had spending power. Teenage girls, especially, were bored with the schoolgirl fantasies peddled by the old-fashioned comics. They wanted magazines of their own, with interviews with pop stars, and articles about clothes and marriage.*

2 *The most important thing in a teenage girl's life was her boyfriend, for whom the clean-cut young boys in pop groups were surrogates. Comic strips made romantic fantasies more accessible.*

3 *A spread from* Hullabaloo. *The magazine started life as a mainstream American teeny pop publication but as the decade advanced, the editorial content changed to embrace the drug culture. By 1968, articles about the Monkees jostled with features on Jefferson Airplane.*

4 *Pictures of pop stars were the staple diet of teenage girls' magazines.*

5 *Fuelling the teenage explosion was pop music.* Hit Parade *specialized in reproducing pop lyrics.*

3

4

5

UNDERGROUND PRESS

1 *"Underground" magazines were never "underground". They were sold on the news-stands like everything else – though some of the more conservative newsagents refused to handle them. The London listings magazine* Time Out *started out "underground".*

2 Rolling Stone *did not look revolutionary. But it was "underground" because it dealt with youth issues in a way the traditional press did not.* Rolling Stone *gave space to writers such as Hunter S. Thompson, the ultimate exponent of the New Journalism.*

3 *"Underground" magazines experimented with writing, printing, layout and graphics – especially once the psychedelic revolution was under way. The use of coloured ink for printing text over colour pictures was not uncommon, although the result was often illegible.*

5

4 *Streetsellers stepped in where more cautious newsagents feared to tread. This man is selling the English-language "underground" magazine* IT – *called the* International Times *until* The Times *sued.*

5 *In Britain,* Oz *magazine, first published in 1967, was the leader of the psychedelic underground. Its founder and editor Richard Neville wanted to produce a visually exciting magazine with underground news, controversial interviews and satire. He ended up in court on obscenity charges.*

6 *The print run of* Oz *began at 15,000 and climbed to a very respectable 30,000. The title came from the hippy-approved fantasy movie* The Wizard of Oz – *and from the fact that the editor was Australian. Myriad colours, and words printed in an unreadable pink on red were common devices. The magazine was not supposed to be read – it was to be experienced.*

6

BOOK JACKETS

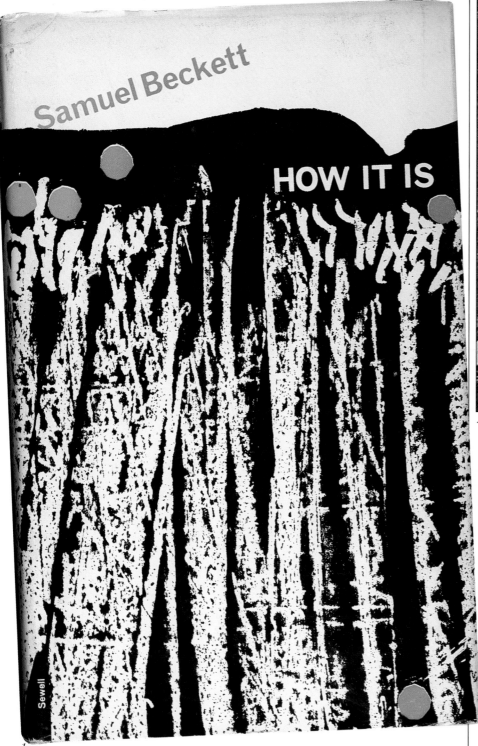

1

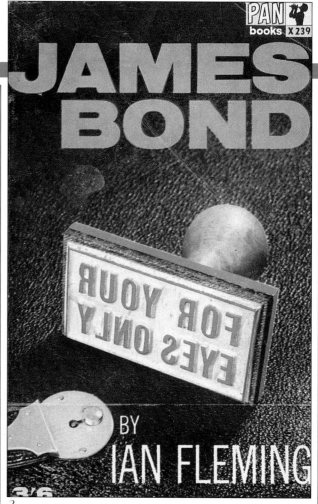

2

3

1 Book jacket designers at publishing houses freed themselves from the shackles of traditional jacket design and left behind the old-fashioned idea of simply using a picture that illustrated the theme of the book. More expressive graphic art devices found favour, especially with leading authors such as Samuel Beckett.

2 James Bond is one of the great fictional figures of the sixties. The simple device of a rubber stamp reverses the letter and produces an eye-catching graphic innovation.

3 The Naked Lunch in which William Burroughs flaunted his promiscuous homosexuality, drug addiction and obsession with hanging, went to the very edge. The cover shockingly echoes pictures from the Nazi death camps – a startling image that no one would have dared use in such a fashion before the sixties.

4 The book of the film – or, in this case, the book of the TV show – took off in the sixties. Literature began to follow the visual media, rather than lead them.

5 Penguin particularly adopted a more radical graphic style during the sixties under the art direction of Germano Facetti.

6 And, of course, there were the Beatles. John Lennon's sub-Goon Show ramblings managed to escape the fan mags and achieve some sort of intellectual respectability through publication by Penguin. Elsewhere toffee-nosed critics were comparing the Fab Four to Mozart.

7 Penguin almost abandoned a house style to find the most apt image for each book. Their logo and a standard grid were all that held their list together.

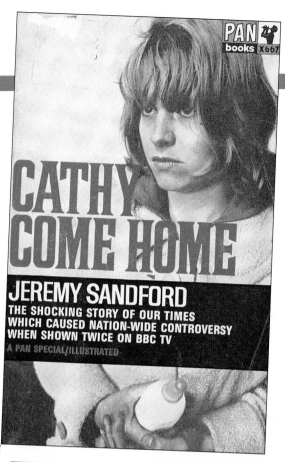

4

6

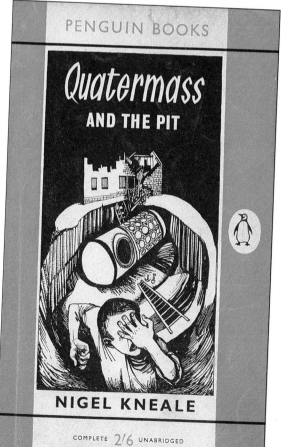

5

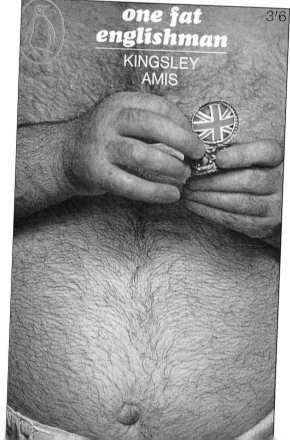

7

RECORD SLEEVES

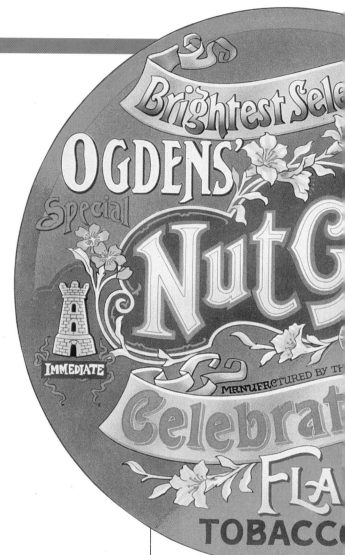

1 *The cover of the Beatles' album* Sergeant Pepper's Lonely Hearts Club Band *had it all. It was designed by pop artist Peter Blake and featured the four members of the group, old-fashioned army uniform, Victorian type styles, famous faces and photomontage.*

2 *Country Joe and the Fish were overtly alternative. In* I Feel Like I'm Fixin' to Die, *they satirized the Vietnam war. The drug influence penetrated further than the graphics though, and in 1969 Country Joe himself was busted for marijuana.*

3 *The ingenious circular cover of the album* Ogden's Nut Gone Flake, *by the Small Faces, won a design award. The problem was that the small, flat paper hinges that held the sleeve together tore easily and the album had to be jammed between regular square covers to stop it rolling off the shelf.*

4 *Cream's debut album featured the members of the group photographed as wax dummies dressed, ironically, as Second World War pilots. The title is pure* Nova.

5 *Robert Crumb was one of the most famous underground cartoonists of the time. His work – which featured sex, drug use and alternative lifestyles – appeared in underground magazines across the world. Here he immortalizes Janis Joplin's band.*

6 *The Who make ironic reference to the advertisements of the day. In 1967, "selling out" was the ultimate sin. The Who were tongue in cheek about that too.*

POSTERS

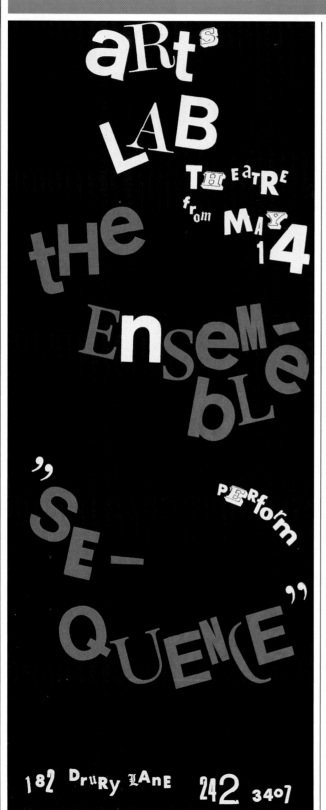

1

2

1 The use of multiple typefaces predated punk. It also helped alienate the elderly.

2 A poster from Fillmore West from a group of artists working out of San Francisco. Illegibility was at a premium. Fat, rounded lettering reached its height in Yellow Submarine in 1968.

3 The dramatic use of simple graphic devices was not the exclusive preserve of rock bands. Politicians found it the perfect tool for getting their message across too.

3

4

5

4 *A poster for a legalize cannabis rally. Counter-culture politicians also used graphics to communicate, but for their purposes the clear unmuddled lines of the early sixties had to be left behind.*

5 *Posters were not just used to advertise an event, an album or a political ideal. They were works of art. They put pop icons on the walls of every hippy pad in the country.*

The Who in Mod gear.

INTRODUCTION

In the sixties, television came of age. Although the flickering tube had been around since the thirties, it had only really been a toy until presidential candidates John F. Kennedy and Richard Milhous Nixon used it to stage their campaign debate in 1961. A year later, Telstar was bouncing TV pictures across the Atlantic and the newly elected President Kennedy was using the all-pervading medium to explain his foreign policy over the Cuban missile crisis and Southeast Asia to the world.

The all-seeing eye
From then on, television simply took over as the medium of mass communication. From a single set with a purple magnifying screen crouched in the corner of the living room, it invaded every room of the house. Rich families bought two or even three sets. Poorer people bought portables so that they could carry them around. And, by the end of the decade, black and white had given way to full living colour.

America, always striving to be an open society, broadcast its space shots live. Few who witnessed it will forget the pictures of men first walking on the moon. The 1964 Tokyo Olympics forced the pace in the race to ring the planet with telecommunication satellites. So by the time the 1968 Mexico Olympics came along, the world was ready to be shocked by Tommy Smith and John Carlos, US medal winners in the 200 metres, giving the Black Power salute – just as it had been shocked when Sheriff Bull Connors had set his police dogs on black schoolchildren protesting for civil rights.

TV also gave the world the assassination of John Kennedy and the live, on-screen murder of his accused assassin Lee Harvey Oswald. The gunshots that wasted Bobby Kennedy – and the desperate attempts to revive him – also made prime time. By the late sixties, you could sit in your living room and watch the Russian tanks roll into Prague, mirror-eyed GIs blasting gooks, and Yippies facing down the "pigs" at the Chicago convention of 1968.

Trial by television
This was not without its consequences. History records that the Americans crushed the Viet Cong in the 1968 Tet offensive, but the image of what the US government had characterized as ill-equipped peasants blasting their way through the elite Marine Corps into the compound of the US Embassy in Saigon convinced America that it could not win the war. Saigon police chief General Nguyen Ngoc Loan – an ally! – blowing the brains out of a Viet Cong suspect without due process did not help matters. And when veteran CBS TV news anchorman Walter Cronkite changed his mind about the war, saying in his nightly opinion piece that the Tet offensive had made it "more certain than ever that the bloody experience of Vietnam is to end in a stalemate", President Johnson privately

lambasted him as a traitor and decided not to run for President again. It was veteran Vietnamese leader Ho Chi Minh – not the Harvard Business School advisors in their polyester suits – who realized that the war in Vietnam would not be won in the paddy fields and jungles of that benighted country but on the TV screens of America.

But television did not just concern itself with such momentous global events. It brought the new pop music to the screen in programmes like *American Bandstand* and the *Ed Sullivan Show* in the USA and *Ready, Steady, Go* and *Top of the Pops* in Britain. And not having any Beatles of its own, America invented *The Monkees*.

As the decade progressed though, pop performances became too outrageous for the small screen (there was no room for Jimi Hendrix on *Ed Sullivan*). Pop music had to find its own mass-media outlets – with pirate radio stations off the coast of Britain and huge open air pop concerts on both sides of the Atlantic.

Rod Serling's *Twilight Zone*, which began in 1959, *The Outer Limits, Dr Who,* and *Star Trek* – the 17 episodes of which have been repeated regularly since – fictionalized the future of the space race. And sixties mysticism was given a further boost by *I Dream of Jeannie* and the very popular *Bewitched*.

A moving comic strip
The Pop Art obsession with comic strips surfaced on the TV screen in *Batman*. But instead of playing it straight – like the fifties series *Superman* – the producers turned the adventures of "the caped crusader" into high camp.

The slick, unmistakably tongue-in-cheek spy image portrayed by James Bond in the cinema was aped on TV by *I Spy, Mission Impossible* and *The Man from U.N.C.L.E.*

1 The adventures of Batman "the caped crusader" and his sidekick Robin were played for laughs.

2 Pictures of astronauts Armstrong and Aldrin walking on the moon were relayed back to Earth to stun TV viewers across the world.

3 David Janssen starred in The Fugitive. *The show won an Emmy award for Best Drama Series in 1965.*

4 Rowan and Martin's Laugh-in, *one of the hits of the late sixties.*

It was likewise sent up in *Get Smart* and marionetted in *Thunderbirds,* where the puppet heroes of International Rescue use the ultimate in James Bond gadgetry to save lives and foil wickedness worldwide. *Danger Man* spy hero Patrick McGoohan fell out with the security forces and found himself trapped in a mysterious village-cum-prison – actually Portmeirion in Wales – in *The Prisoner.* In the series little is explained. McGoohan is questioned by a series of interrogators calling themselves Number 2. They want "information". McGoohan wants to know who Number 1 is. He is told that he is Number 6. The formula was compelling. Twenty years on, *The Prisoner* still has a worldwide fan club, along with the perennial *Star Trek* and *Dr Who.*

Another compelling formula was hit upon in *The Fugitive.* Played by David Janssen, the fugitive was on the run from an avenging policeman for the murder of his wife. In turn, he was on the trail of a one-armed man who he believed was the real murderer. This gave Janssen the chance to turn up in a new community each week, do good, then move on.

Transatlantic Man

The sixties witnessed the beginning of the irresistible rise of David Frost. He began his TV career by hosting a mini-series on the dance craze *The Twist* but came to prominence in England MCing the late-night satire show *That Was The Week That Was.* The ease of jet travel and his mid-Atlantic manner allowed him to commute between London and New York, establishing himself as an American talk-show host while continuing to front the mild-mannered satire shows *The Frost Report* and *Frost Over England* in Britain. In *The Frost Programme,* he turned himself briefly into TV's most aggressive interviewer, conducting a lethal "trial by television" of the former British fascist leader Oswald Mosley and others.

Frost also produced the aggressively funny *At Last the 1948 Show* starring John Cleese, who had appeared with Frost in *The Frost Report.* In 1969, *At Last the 1948 Show* evolved into the cult *Monty Python's Flying Circus.*

In America, scriptwriters – like those portrayed in the enormously successful *Dick Van Dyke Show* in the early sixties – tripped out on acid in 1967 to come up with the ultimate sixties comedy show *Rowan and Martin's Laugh-in.* Psychedelic sets, hip catchphrases and relentless pace won it Emmys in 1967 and 1968 for Best Variety Show. By 1977, when it was revived, it was hopelessly out of date and sank without a trace.

But TV was not just a medium for comedy, music and mindless pap. Drama series – most notably the BBC's *Wednesday Play* – tackled serious social issues like homelessness, mental breakdown and alcoholism. In keeping with the spirit of the times, the plays had their share of offensive language and gratuitous nudity.

155

1

1 Cleopatra *was an appropriate movie to herald the new age. It was the last of the great historical spectaculars. A study of a liberated woman, it spoke volumes about the power of sex. The sparks struck between Elizabeth Taylor and Richard Burton on screen spilled over into their private lives. For the first time, movies stars were openly, unashamedly committing infidelity and all the world did was applaud. The sixties had really begun.*

2 The stars of the French New Wave eventually made their way to Hollywood. Not only did Brigitte Bardot and Jeanne Moreau grab the attention of English-speaking audiences, the director Louis Malle – a celebrated French Nouvelle Vague auteur – also made an impression in the home of the English-speaking cinema.*

3 The Graduate *broke new ground in 1967. Never had sex – and a complex sexual situation – been handled so frankly in a mainstream movie. It also introduced actor Dustin Hoffman and the music of Simon and Garfunkel to cinema audiences.*

The Epic and beyond

Competition from TV also had its effect on the movies. By 1963 the Hollywood studio system had finally broken down, but that did not mean there would be no more spectaculars. *West Side Story* came to the big screen in 1961. Elizabeth Taylor and Richard Burton began their romance on and off screen in the 1963 production of *Cleopatra*. Steve McQueen tried his heroic leap to freedom in *The Great Escape* in 1963. Stanley Baker and Michael Caine made their fruitless stand in *Zulu* in 1964. Alfred Hitchcock produced *Psycho* in 1960 and *The Birds* in 1963, while David Lean came up with *Lawrence of Arabia* in 1962 and *Dr Zhivago* in 1965.

In France, the New Wave was still breaking, with François Truffaut, Claude Chabrol, Jean-Luc Godard and others revolutionizing the way films were made. Alain Resnais directed the intellectual hit *Last Year in Marienbad* in 1961. What really happened "last year in Marienbad" is still a matter of debate, as even the director and writer do not agree.

Some of the stars of the New Wave – notably Brigitte Bardot and Catherine Deneuve – went on to surf across a wider screen. Director Roger Vadim also escaped to Hollywood, where he directed the soft-porn sci-fi spoof *Barbarella,* starring Jane Fonda.

Veteran Spanish surrealist Luis Buñuel used Catherine Deneuve in 1967 in his most mainstream picture *Belle de Jour* – the story of a frigid housewife who spends her afternoons as a prostitute. From the Polish film school came Roman Polanski whose demonic *Rosemary's Baby* was tragically echoed in his own life when Charles Manson's "Family" slaughtered the director's pregnant wife Sharon Tate and three friends at a party at their Beverly Hills home.

From Italy, Federico Fellini and Michelangelo Antonioni rose to international fame in 1960 with *La Dolce Vita* and *L'Avventura,* respectively. In 1961, Paolo Pasolini made his debut with *Accatone,* followed in 1962 by Bernardo Bertolucci with *La Commare Secca*.

Western dance was also much invigorated by the defection of Russian ballet star Rudolf Nureyev in 1961. Only a week after his defection, he made his debut with the Paris Opera in *Sleeping Beauty*.

The swinging city

Antonioni went on to make the ultimate "swinging London" picture *Blow-Up* in 1966, with David Hemmings playing the chic symbol of the day, a fashion photographer, whose lifestyle was loosely based on that of David Bailey.

The swingingness of London was also examined in *Morgan – A Suitable Case for Treatment, Georgy Girl,* Dick Lester's *The Knack* and his zany Beatles films *Hard Day's Night* and *Help!* The Beatles also blazed a trail with their psychedelic feature-length cartoon *Yellow Submarine* and their equally mind-expanding, yet rather self-indulgent, *Magical Mystery Tour.* Bob Dylan took to the screen in the enigmatic *Don't Look Back.* Mick Jagger turned serious actor in *Performance* and *Ned Kelly,* both released in 1970. Ringo Starr turned up with Peter Sellers in the weird and wonderful *Magic Christian,* but the wackiest film of the decade must have been *What's New Pussycat,* written by Woody Allen, with Peter Sellers playing a demented psychiatrist and Peter O'Toole a relentless womanizer.

Sex, a perpetual topic of the sixties, reared its beautiful head in the movies – from the innocent look back at an era of easy permissiveness in *Tom Jones,* through *Here We Go Round the Mulberry Bush,* to Sweden's *I Am Curious Yellow.* Sex also became the staple of the cinema of the counter-culture, America's underground. Andy Warhol made *Flesh* and *Chelsea Girls.* But he, and others in the underground, often simply preferred to bore the pants off people.

Violence also got a look in with Sam Peckinpah's *The Wild Bunch,* Don Siegel's filming of the Hemingway short story *The Killers,* starring Lee Marvin and Ronald Reagan, Arthur Penn's *Bonnie and Clyde* and a fistful of spaghetti westerns directed by Sergio Leone.

The cult of youth

But youth was the thing. College students rebelled in *Strawberry Statement.* The young audience laughed to see the ageing John Wayne waste the gooks in *The Green Berets,* the only picture where the sun sets in the east. They had to wait for the more eloquent anti-war statements of *M.A.S.H.* and *Catch 22* to see their own pacifist viewpoint expressed.

But the movie that most caught the imagination of youth in those disaffected days was *Easy Rider.* Made in 1969, it had it all – motorbikes, music, drugs and death – the mindless murder of misunderstood youth, of course.

2

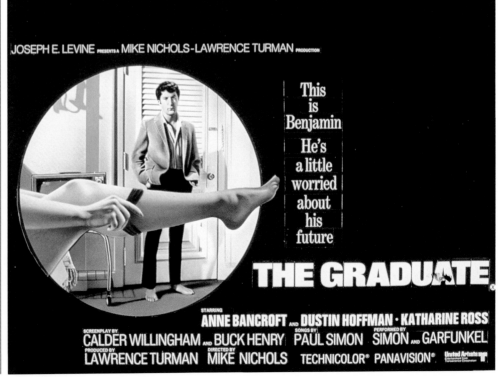

INSPIRATIONS

1

3

1 This sadhu or Nepalese holy man has the love beads, the kaftan, the long hair, the beard and the headband that quickly came to constitute the hippy image so beloved of TV and the movies.

2 You did not have to be conspicuously young or trendy to host American Bandstand, a pop music show. Dick Clark certainly was not. Even at the time, he looked like a doting parent or an indulgent uncle who let the kids get on with it in the sure and certain knowledge that they would come back to Frank Sinatra in the end. They did not, and they learnt to hate Dick Clark, too.

3 The dance steps in sixties' movies and pop programmes were the same, but not necessarily done in unison as they were in Gold Diggers of 1935.

2

4 Black Southern Baptist churches produced many of the finest singers of the sixties. And if you were not lucky enough or, in those days especially, unlucky enough – to be born black, you listened to spirituals and stole what you could.

4

5 Elvis, of course, was still king, though many thought he was not the same since he had been in the army. He gradually turned his back on rock 'n' roll, saying that he had never liked it anyway and preferred ballads. His ambition had always been to be a Hollywood star like Marlon Brando or James Dean.

6 The Brooklyn Paramount was the first New York home for rock 'n' roll in the late fifties. By the early sixties it had taken the city by storm and by the time the Beatles turned up in 1964 they had to hire Shea Stadium.

7

7 Was she a woman in men's clothing or was she a man in drag, what with that deep voice and all? Androgyny was in in the sixties.

5

6

CURRENT EVENTS

1 The assassination of President John F. Kennedy, as reported by the Honolulu Star-Bulletin, 22 November, 1963. Every newspaper around the world had the same headline that day.

2 An amateur photographer made a movie that showed the moment the bullets hit Kennedy. Soon it was being screened by every TV station in the world.

3 President Kennedy had met his Russian opposite number, Soviet Premier Nikita Khrushchev, at their summit in Vienna, on 3 June, 1961. Kennedy warned Khrushchev that America had twice gone to war to protect western Europe. They disagreed about Berlin but were in accord about Laos, guaranteeing its sovereignty. The following year Kennedy sent troops there and the two leaders were facing each other down over Cuba.

160

4 *In America's Deep South, blacks – still known as negroes then – fought for their civil rights. They had been denied the right to vote, to equal education, to decent housing – even the right to eat at "whites only" lunch counters. Blacks were not allowed to sit at the front of buses if a white wanted to sit there, and had to use segregated lavatories. And when blacks protested at these injustices, the police responded with dogs and clubs. When pictures like this were seen on TV in the liberal North and in Europe, public opinion forced change.*

5 *The Vietnam War was not popular anywhere. America – a massively rich superpower – seemed to be picking on one of the poorest, most backward countries in the world. American youth rebelled because they did not want to fight. European youth protested because they did not want their countries to get involved. One of the largest demonstrations took place outside the American Embassy in London's Grosvenor Square in 1968.*

6 *Richard Nixon lost the contest for the presidency to Kennedy in 1960, then failed in his bid to become Governor of California in 1962 because of his poor TV image. But by 1968 he was back, seizing the presidency on the promise to stop the war in Vietnam.*

4

5

6

161

EARLY POP MUSIC

1 *Promo pic of the clean-cut kids of Californian pop, the Beach Boys, with the signature of Mike Love. Like other bands, some of them eventually got into the sex, drugs and rock 'n' roll scene. Mike Love was also into transcendental meditation.*

2 *Pet Sounds, the Beach Boys seminal album.*

3 *Bob Zimmerman took the name of a poet and himself became the poet of Pop. Although his early work had more in common with the style of the protest songs of thirties' folk singers, eventually he could resist it no longer and, in 1965, went electric. The meaning of his rambling lyrics was discussed by stoned pseudo-intellectuals everywhere.*

4 *The Beatles were the sixties. They were formed in 1959 as a leather-clad group of rockers. In 1962, they went Mod and came to London. In 1964, they took style to the USA. In return they got into drugs, transcendental meditation, love, peace and hippydom. Their lyrics even inspired the murders of Charles Manson's "family" on which chilling note the decade ended. In 1970, they broke up.*

4

6

5 The Rolling Stones were the bad boys of rock. While the girls went for the good looks of the Beatles, the boys went for the Rolling Stones for their appalling behaviour. Even by the late sixties, the Rolling Stones had begun calling themselves "the greatest rock and roll band in the world". Few have ever challenged them.

6 *Otis Redding brought Soul to a white audience. If "white niggers" like Elvis Presley had, in the fifties, been the first to make whites more aware of Black music, Black singers were then still confining themselves to "race records" and using white singers to help mass market their songs. Black singers could now sell their own songs to everyone.*

5

LATE POP MUSIC

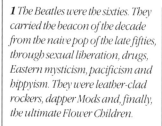

1 *The Beatles were the sixties. They carried the beacon of the decade from the naïve pop of the late fifties, through sexual liberation, drugs, Eastern mysticism, pacificism and hippyism. They were leather-clad rockers, dapper Mods and, finally, the ultimate Flower Children.*

2 *Arthur Brown's only hit record, Fire, reached number two in the charts in Britain in 1967. Brown's eccentric act was the precursor of the theatrical rock of the seventies and eighties. His band, The Crazy World of Arthur Brown, included drummer Carl Palmer, later of Emerson, Lake and Palmer, and Vincent Crane of Atomic Rooster.*

3 *Janis Joplin brought the sound of white blues to the sixties. From Port Arthur, Texas, Joplin, with her band Big Brother and the Holding Company, stopped the show at the Monterey Pop Festival in 1967. Her gutsy style was given extra edge by her ill-concealed vulnerability. Her sex life, her boozing and her drug problem were legendary.*

4

5

6

4 Jefferson Airplane were the sound of Haight Ashbury. They brought San Francisco psychedelia to the world.

5 The close harmony of the Mamas and the Papas brought a Flower Power sound to America's east coast.

6 Jim Morrison's ramblings sounded eerily profound when backed by the dry organ and jazzy guitar of The Doors.

165

HAPPENINGS AND CONCERTS

2nd i o w festival of music friday	2nd i o w festival of music sat	2nd i o w festival of music sunday
the nice	**the who**	**bob dylan**
bonzo dog band	moody blues	**the band**
eclection	fat mattress	**richie havens**
edgar broughton	family	julie felix
free	marsha hunt	third ear band
blonde on blonde	and white trash	pentangle
gypsy	pretty things	tom paxton
heaven	blodwyn pig	gary farr
	aynsley dunbar	indo jazz fusions
	king crimson	liverpool scene
	joe cocker	

1 Huge outdoor pop festivals were the invention of the sixties. They were less to do with music appreciation – usually the stage was so far away that it was difficult to hear the bands anyway – and more to do with an explosion of collective consciousness. Europe's biggest ever outdoor festival was held at the Isle of Wight.

2 Sympathetic participants in a "happening" are inundated with soap suds. Life was supposed to be fun. Only squares failed to dig that.

3 Woodstock was the biggest festival of them all – three days of love and peace that were supposed to be the birth of a new nation. In fact, it was the death-knell of the hippy dream.

4 *The sun was supposed to shine. You could take your clothes off among like-minded people. Drugs were freely available. There would be music. The talk would be of peace and love, harmony and universal brotherhood. Young people were taking over and the world would be a better place for it. There would be no Cold War when there was free love. Capitalism or Communism made no difference. The oppressed peoples of the Third World would be liberated by our philosophy. It all sounded so good, out there in the sunshine. But maybe it was just the dope talking.*

5 *The Rolling Stones used free concerts skilfully to promote themselves. Their first was in London's Hyde Park where Mick Jagger wore one of Marianne Faithfull's dresses. The last was at Altamont.*

6 *The ultimate outdoor happening was the "love-in". And the weirder and more whacked out you looked, the better. If you painted your face and danced in a strange way, people assumed you were in touch with a higher plane of consciousness. This "love-in" took place in the grounds of the English stately home Woburn Abbey in the Summer of Love, 1967.*

5

6

4

POP ON TV AND FILM

1 Pop invades TV. America, failing to come up with its own Beatles, decided to manufacture a group. NBC put together Englishman David Jones with Peter Tork, Mickey Dolenz and Mike Nesmith to form the Monkees, in their own TV show. This even employed the whacky cinematic tricks that Dick Lester had used in the Beatles' movies.

2 Cliff Richard and friends take a Summer Holiday in 1963. The film, as innocuous and inoffensive as it was possible, was the first of the British pop movies.

3 In Alice's Restuarant, the folk singer Arlo Guthrie – son of the legendary Woody Guthrie – tries to get it together in a hippy utopia. Director Arthur Penn takes the cynical approach, though, and splits the group up in the end.

4 How could the Beatles go wrong? They brought Black American music and northern charm to Swinging London, where director Dick Lester put them in a stylish vehicle which showed off all their talents. Their first film, A Hard Day's Night, *became a classic of the period.*

5 Simon and Garfunkel appeared in person in Monterey Pop *(1968) – a forerunner of the classic* Woodstock. *But they are remembered better for their soundtrack to* The Graduate *(1967).*

COMEDY ON TV AND FILM

1

2

Peter Sellers · George C.

In Stanley Kubrick's

Dr. Strangelov

Or:
How
I Learned
To
Stop
Worrying
And
Love
The
Bomb

the hot line suspense com

also starring Sterling Hayden · Keenan Wynn · Slim Pickens *and introducing* Tracy Reed *as* "Miss Foreign Affairs"   Screenplay by St

Produced and Directed by Stanley Kubrick   A Columbia

3

1 *The Bonzo Dog Doo-Dah Band was one of the whackiest groups of the sixties. Although their music owed more to jazz – and their approach more to Dada – their 1968 "top five" hit in Britain (*I'm the Urban Spaceman*) earned them a place on the BBC's* Top of the Pops.

2 *The TV comedy series* Monty Python's Flying Circus *started in 1969. It owed much to the anarchic humour of Spike Milligan's radio* Goon Show *in combining highbrow wit with delicious bad taste.*

3 *The great comedy actor Peter Sellers plays three roles in* Dr Strangelove, *hilariously. Based on the novel by Terry Southern, the film, directed by Stanley Kubrick, turns atomic warfare – the most serious subject of the decade – into pure and telling farce.*

ick, Peter George and Terry Southern

4 *Beautiful downtown Burbank turned on to hippy humour in 1967 with* Rowan and Martin's Laugh-In. *Dan Rowan and Dick Martin were the slightly establishment, tuxedoed ringmasters of this quick-fire sketch and gag show. What kept it running were the catchphrases. These included: "Sock it to me"; "You bet your sweet hippy"; "Look it up in your Funk and Wagnalls"; "Very interesting, but stupid"; and "Here comes de judge".*

YOUTH FILM

1 *One way of attracting the youth audience was to have a pop star in your film. In* Performance, *1967, Mick Jagger plays a reclusive rock star with an identity problem. Permissive sex was also de rigueur in youth films.*

2 *Youthful, but hardly harmless, rebellion came to the public school in Lindsay Anderson's* If, *1968.*

3 *Malcolm McDowell made his screen debut as Mick Travis in* If. *He has remained director Lindsay Anderson's favourite leading man ever since.*

4 *Elvis Presley made his film debut in 1956 with* Love Me Tender *and he had made four movies by the time he was drafted into the army in 1958. When he was discharged in March 1960 the deal was already sealed for him to relive his army experiences for the big screen in* GI Blues, *which was released in October of that year.*

5 *Coming at the end of the decade,* Easy Rider *(1969) had all the ingredients that summed up the experience of being young in the sixties – motor bikes, drugs, permissive sex, alternative lifestyles, adolescent rebellion and early, violent death.*

4

5

NEW WAVE

1 *Jean Seberg and Jean-Paul Belmondo in* Au Bout de Souffle (Breathless). *Directed by Jean-Luc Godard it went on release early in the sixties. Godard also took away the breath of the critics with his revolutionary use of the jump-cut to give an almost metaphysical dimension to this "new-wave" reappraisal of the Hollywood thriller.*

2 *Marcello Mastroianni in Federico Fellini's* 8½ *released in 1963. The title of this largely autobiographical film refers to the number of films that the master of the Italian "new wave" had made up until then.*

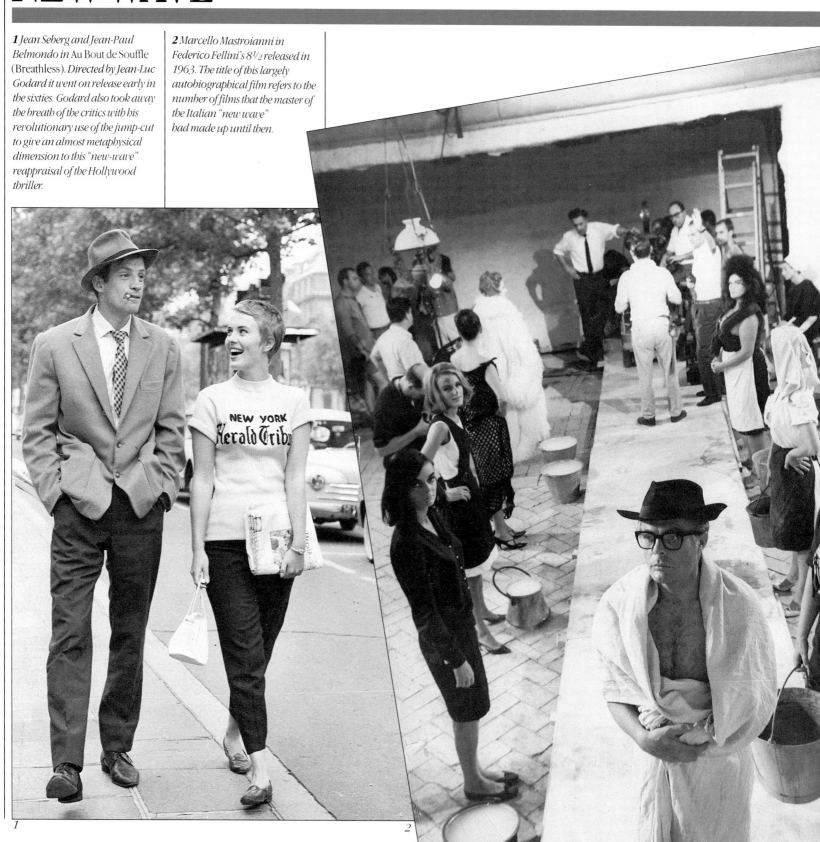

1

2

3 *The 1961 film* Last Year in Marienbad, *directed by Alain Resnais, is one of the most deliberately confusing films of all time. It deals with the complex problems posed by time itself.*

4 *The British "new wave" largely sprang from the theatrical and literary work of the Angry Young Men of the fifties. John Osborne's* Look Back in Anger *was filmed by Tony Richardson and provided the perfect vehicle for the young Richard Burton.*

5 *Alan Sillitoe's grim novel of life and love in working-class northern England,* Saturday Night and Sunday Morning, *was filmed by Karel Reisz in 1960.*

3

4

5

UNDERGROUND FILM

1 *As well as directing films himself, Andy Warhol backed other underground enterprises. Paul Morrissey directed most of The Factory's later output. Flesh (1968) was the first of the batch of Morrissey's more commercially oriented movies. It made Joe Dallesandro something of an underground film star.*

2 *Andy Warhol's Chelsea Girls (1966) comes with a complicated set of instructions of how and when to lace each reel into the projector. Each reel is a single take. There is a lot of zooming and focusing, but no narrative.*

1

2

3 Made by the Italian "new wave" director, Michelangelo Antonioni, on his way to Hollywood, Blow-Up is set in Swinging London's world of fashion and photography. The film is not generally considered "underground", although Antonioni borrows many underground techniques – notably that of having an unfathomable plot line.

4 The French nouvelle vague was largely a literary movement. But members who were radical-left anti-capitalists came to see themselves as underground film directors. Jean-Luc Godard, perhaps the best known of the French "new wave" film-makers, had the best of both worlds. He worked for the state-owned TV, but explained that he did so only to earn money to create "a more revolutionary product".

SCI-FI AND SPIES

1

3

2

1 The Man From Uncle *brought James Bond-style shenanigans to TV. UNCLE was obviously an avuncular free-world agency, while its arch-enemy SMERSH was a ruthless totalitarian outfit. But the series' Cold War message had its tongue planted firmly in its cheek. It ran from 1967 to 1969.*

2 The Avengers *was shown on British TV throughout the sixties. It was a zany romp through Swinging London, starring Patrick McNee as a dandified secret agent and a series of pistol-packing, karate-capering, trendily attired dolly birds.*

3 Barbarella *brought soft-porn sci-fi to the silver screen. The director Roger Vadim had already made Brigitte Bardot an international sex symbol. Here he works the same magic on his new love Jane Fonda in 1968. David Hemmings brought all the trendiness of Blow Up with him to the production. And the fixtures, fittings and fantasies of the movie all proved to be influential in everyday life.*

4

4 Thunderbirds are go! The puppetry may be a little stiff but the situations and characters – all familiar from the world of James Bond – were so well drawn that the programme was enjoyed by adults and children alike. It was first shown in 1966.

5 The original series of Star Trek ran for just two years, from 1966 to 1968. But Scotty's transporters, Ohura's legs and Mr Spock's pointed ears assured it a cult following.

5

6 Dr Who has been unstoppable. It has run, on and off, since 1963. The Doctor's favourite opponents are the Daleks. They are supposed to be so deformed and hideous that they have to live inside these mechanical outfits.

6

SEX AND VIOLENCE

1

2

1 *There is not much sex in* Bonnie and Clyde – *Clyde Barrow was impotent, but Arthur Penn's climax with Faye Dunaway and Warren Beatty's bodies being riddled with bullets in slow motion was one of the most violent scenes ever filmed.*

2 Rosemary's Baby *was Polish director Roman Polanski's first Hollywood film. He had brought with him from Europe a fascination with the absurd and the surreal – especially in the portrayal of frightening and violent situations.*

3 *Sixties' directors tried to portray the truth of the Wild West with all its violent excesses. John Sturges found that he could do this by importing the bloodsoaked plot of Askira Kurosawa's* The Seven Samurai.

3

6

4

4 Roger Vadim had already turned Brigitte Bardot into an international sex symbol. In Barbarella he made his new love Jane Fonda into another Vadim heroine, infinitely attractive and infinitely available.

5 After his success in the long-running TV cowboy series Rawhide, Clint Eastwood quit the US to make Spaghetti Westerns with Sergio Leone. They were violent parodies of Hollywood Westerns, made mainly in Spain.

6 Sex reared its beautiful head. Gratuitous nudity and explicit sex scenes were used in underground films and even in legitimate Hollywood productions if the producers thought there was the slightest chance they could get away with it. In Germany and Scandinavia no excuses were needed for undressing on film.

5

DANCE

1

2

1 In the sixties there was a great explosion in ballet. London's Royal Ballet especially was at its height. Here Kenneth MacMillan's piece Brandenburg *is being performed in 1967. Now called* Concerto, *it is still part of the Royal Ballet's repertoire.*

2 Margot Fonteyn was at the height of her powers. Here she is dancing the original Russian version of Swan Lake, *introduced to the Royal Ballet in the sixties by Frederick Ashton.*

3 In the sixties, ballet became an international business. Here, the Alwin Nikolais Ballet dance the Mantis scene from Imago *at London's Sadlers Wells in 1969, establishing the American company on the world stage.*

4 The defection of Rudolf Nureyev was crucial. Before he brought his muscular artistry to the West, male dancers were little more than leaning posts. He set male dancers on a new course. Here he is dancing Frederick Ashton's Birthday Offering *in 1968 with Margot Fonteyn.*

4

3

THEATER AND MUSICALS

1 Mysteries and Other Pieces *by the archetypal underground group, the Living Theatre in Montmartre, Paris, in 1967. The play took the audience through the death experience. Here the actors transcend death and celebrate the oneness of the universe by chanting – along with the audience – "Om".*

2 Moliére's Tartuffe *was staged by the National Theatre company at London's Old Vic in 1968. The decade saw the realization of a dream – the birth of a National Theatre in Britain, which had been an ambition for over a century.*

3 With the musical Hair, *the underground theatre – gratuitous nudity and all – joined with pop music to invade New York's Broadway and London's West End. Even the old guard saw it as revolutionary. The ultra-liberated* Oh! Calcutta *followed, but that was the end of the short-lived theatrical challenge of the underground.*

4 The poster for Hair *proclaims its hippy philosophy and its drug inspiration.*

january 1968 incorporating theatre world & encore 4s

plays
and players

Full text of
David Pinner's
FANGHORN

Row on TV over Hair

By Daily Mail Reporter

ZSA ZSA GABOR turned Eamonn Andrews's new ITV show into farce last night.

She was one of Eamonn's guests on stage at the Shaftesbury Theatre.

Part of the musical *Hair* which opens at the theatre tonight, was to be televised as a finale to the programme.

In the chat before the musical excerpt Miss Gabor started to go on about long hair . . . with the long-haired cast of *Hair* looking on.

As she continued about 'real acting' a voice from the back of the hall shouted : 'You are not a real actress.'

Zsa Zsa complained to Mr Andrews that she had been insulted. She invited the man to come up. He did.

He was American Bertrand Castelli, who produced *Hair* in New York.

She stalked off, stumbled, and fell into the arms of some of the cast of *Hair*. They carried her back on stage chanting 'We love you Zsa Zsa.'

Then the number *Aquarius* was televised. Originally it was planned to show a scene in which some of the play appear nude — but the refused.

3

4

185

INDEX

190

CREDITS

Quarto would like to thank the following for their help with this publication and for permission to reproduce copyright material.

© ADAGP, Paris and DACS, London 1989. *Gino Severini, Centrifugal Expansion of Light*: p46 (4); *Arcaid/Richard Einzig*: pp20, 22/23, 30/31 (2c) (5c), 32/33 (2c) (3c) (4c) (6c), 34/35 (1c) (6c), 108/109 (2c) (4c), 112/113 (4c), 120/121 (1c) (2) (3); *Arcaid/Vivienne Porter*: pp32/33 (7c); *Architectural Association/Ross Feller*: pp30/31 (8c); *Architectural Association/Jim Monahan*: pp34/35 (2c); *Architectural Association/ Ingrid Morris*: pp30/31 (4c); *Architectural Association/Geoff Smythe*: pp34/35 (4c); *Architectural Association/ Harry Urena*: pp22/23; *Architectural Association/Robert Vickery*: pp34/35 (3c); *Archigram Group/Ron Herron and Warren Chalk*: pp36/37 (1c) (2) (3) (4) (5c); *Austin Rover*: pp96/97 (6); © *BACS 1989 Victor Vasarely Banya*: pp68/69 (6); © *Peter Blake 1989*: p48 (2); *Black Star Colorific/Charles Moore*: pp160/161 (4c); *Black Star Colorific/Arthur Rickerby*: pp10/11 (1c); *Black Star Colorific/Fred Ward*: pp10/11 (5c); *Black Star Colorific/Werner Wolff*: pp14/15 (4); © *Sir Alan Bowness*: pp52/53 (1) (5); Bridgeman Art Library; © *David Hockney 1964* pp42/43, 44/45 (2), *Bridgeman Art Library*: pp 48/49 (1) (2) (3); *British Aerospace*: pp94/95 (1) (3) (4) (6); *British Film Institute*: pp158/159 (2) (3), 180/182 (6); *Jack Buchan*: pp68/69 (2); *Jack Buchan* © *Time Out*: pp144/145; *Central Press Photos Ltd*: pp14/15 (3); *Moira Clinch*: p27 (5); © *DACS 1989 Roy Lichtenstein* pp40, 44/45 (1); © *DACS 1989 Claes Oldenburg*: pp52 (4); © *DACS 1989 Tom Wesselmann*: pp50; (1); *Design Council*: pp112/113 (3); *Paul Forrester*: pp92/93 (4) *General Motors*: pp96/97 (1); © *David Hockney 1963/'Two Men in a Shower'*: pp48 (3); *Angelo Hornak Collection*: pp28/29 (1) (2) (4), 30/31 (1) (3) (6) (7), 32/33 (1) (5), 52/53 (1) (2), 114/115 (2) (3) (5), 192; *IBM UK LTD*: pp92/93

(1) (2) (3) (5) (6); © *Allen Jones*: pp46/47 (5); *The Keystone Collection*: pp10/11 (3), 12/13 (2), 14/15 (2), 15/16 (3) (4), 22/23, 34/35 (5), 60/61 (4), 72/73 (3) (5), 82/83 (3), 84/85 (2); *The Kobal Collection*: pp86/87 (3) (5), 128/129 (6), 154/155 (1) (3), 158/159 (7), 166, 167 (3), 168/169 (2) (4), 170/171 (3), 172/173 (3) (4), 174/175 (1) (2) (3) (4) (5), 176/177 (1) (2) (3), 178/179 (1) (3) (5), 180/181 (1) (2) (3) (4); *Look Magazine*: pp46/47 (2) (3); *Magnum*: pp18/19 (1) (3), 128/129 (7); *Magnum/Rue Barri*: pp26/27 *Magnum/David Hurn*: pp160/161 (6c), 166/167 (2c); *Magnum/Don McCullin*: pp132/133 (2c), (3c), 164/165 (1); *NASA*: pp86/87 (6) (7), 88/89 (2), 90/91 (1) (2) (3) (5), 154/155 (2); *Novosti*: pp98/99 (3); *Oz magazine*: pp 144/145 (3) (6); *Robert Opie Collection*: pp46 (1), 115 (4); *Tim Page*: pp132/133 (1) (5), 184/185 (1) (2) (3) (4); *Reproduced by kind permission Pan Books, 1989/'For Your Eyes Only' by Ian Fleming*: pp146/147 (2); *Reproduced by kind permission Pan Books 1989/'Cathy Come Home' by Jeremy Sandford*: pp146/147 (5); © *Penguin Books Ltd 1966/'The Penguin John Lennon' by John Lennon*: pp146/147 (6); © *Penguin Books Ltd 1966/'Quatermass and the Pit' by Nigel Kneale*: pp 146/147 (5); © *Penguin Books Ltd 1966/'One fat Englishman' by Kingsley Amis*: pp146/147 (7); *The Photo Source*: pp68/69 (5) *The John Platt Collection*: pp122/123 (1), 126/127 (1) (2) (3), 142/143 (3), (5), 150/151 (2), 164/165 (3) (4) (6); *Playboy 1967*: pp124/125 (3); © *Plays and Players magazine Jan 1968*: pp184/185; *Popperfoto*: pp10/11 (2), 15/16 (2), 26/27 (1), 38/39 (1) (2) (3) (4) (5), 58/59 (3), 64/65 (1) (2) (3) (5), 66/67 (2) (4), 68/69 (1), 78/79 (1) (2) (3) (4) (7) (8), 88/89 (1), 100/101 (1) (3) (4) (5) (6), 116/117 (2), 120/121 (4), 126/127 (4), 128/129 (4), 166/167 (1c) (5)

(6), 168/169 (1), 178/179 (2); *RCA*: pp158/159 (5); © *Rolling Stone magazine*: pp144/145 (2); *Salamander Books Ltd*: p99 (4); *Sony*: pp102/103 (1) (2) (5); *Sothebys*: pp10/11 (4); *Student Magazine*: pp144/145 (3) (5) (6), 176/177 (4); *The Sunday Times*: pp44/45 (1), 60/61 (5); © *Syndication International*: pp184/185 (3); *The Tate Gallery*: 52/53 (4), (5), 54/55 (1) (3); *The Tate Gallery* © *Derek Boshier 1962*: pp42/43; *The Tate Gallery* © *The Henry Moore Foundation 1989* pp46/47; *The Daily Telegraph*: pp12/13 (1); *Telegraph Colour Library*: pp58/59 (1) (2) 60/61 (3), 66/67 (1), 68/69 (3) (4), 70/71 (1) (2) (4) (6), 74/75 (6), 78/79 (5), 118/119 (4), 130/131 (2) (3) (4) (5) (6), 144/145 (4), 180/181 (5); *Telegraph Colour Library/ D. Franklin*: pp42/43; *Topham*: pp2, 5, 10/11 (6), 12/13 (3), 14/15 (1) (5), 15/16 (1), 18/19 (2), 28/29 (3) (6), 44/45 (3), 48/49 (1c) (3c), 52/53 (3), 58/59 (4) (5) (6), 60/61 (1) (2), 62/63 (2) (4) (6), 64/65 (4) (6) (8), 70/71 (3) (5), 72/73 (1) (2) (4), 74/75 (2) (3) (4) (5), 76/77 (6), 78/79 (6) (9), 80, 82/83 (1) (2), 84/85 (1), 90/91 (4), 94/95 (2) (5), 100/101 (2) (4), 102/103 (3) (4), 104, 106/107 (1) (2) (3), 108/109 (3), 112/113 (1) (2) (5) (6), 116/117 (1) (3) (4) (5), 118/119 (1) (2) (3), 124/125 (2), 130/131 (1), 136/137 (1) (2) (5), 146/147 (1) (3), 150/151 (1) (3) (4) (5), 154/155 (2) 158/159 (1) (4), 160/161 (1) (2) (3) (5), 164/165 (2), 170/171 (1) (2), 178/179 (4) (6); *The Vintage Magazine Co*: pp134/135 (1) (3) (4) (5), 142/143 (1) (2) (4); *Reg Wilson*: pp182/183 (1) (2) (3) (4)

Every effort has been made to trace and acknowledge all copyright holders. Quarto would like to apologize if any omissions have been made.

"The dream is over."

JOHN LENNON